TH**INQ** 4-6

Inquiry-based learning
in the junior classroom

Jill Colyer and Jennifer Watt

Published in Canada by Wave Learning Solutions Inc.
617 Logan Ave.
Toronto, ON, Canada, M4K 3C2
email: contact@wavelearningsolutions.com
phone: 1-800-314-4644
website: www.wavelearningsolutions.com

Printed and bound in Canada

1 2 3 4 – 19 18 17 16

ISBN 978-0-99-500180-0

Library and Archives Canada Cataloguing in Publication
Colyer, Jill, author

   THINQ 4-6 : inquiry-based learning in the junior classroom
/ Jill Colyer and Jennifer Watt.

ISBN 978-0-9950018-0-0 (paperback)

   1. Inquiry-based learning. 2. Education, Elementary.
I. Watt, Jennifer Gail, 1965–, author II. Title.

LB1027.23.C64 2016   371.39   C2016-901181-X

Publisher: David Steele
Production editor: Laura Kim
Formatter: Janette Thompson (Jansom)
Technical support: Emma Steele

CONTENTS

FOREWORD

One of the most surprising things about the world of education is how so few individuals actually know the "beginnings" of the primary and secondary school structure. Invented in the late 19th century, the focus was to develop a literate workforce. Standardization was the common denominator and from standardization came specialization. This model of learning served societies well and unprecedented wealth was generated. Fortunately, we have seen much evolution in our society but nothing more significant than our emerging consciousness of the world around us.

From the time I began teaching in 1976, indicators of success highlighted the need to be able to articulate one's thoughts, primarily via the pen, and integrate all the needed "skills" to be successful. Such "skills" development remains important yet we now know that given this increased consciousness, it can only bring us so far. From the emerging research about the brain and the relationship to student intellectual engagement, to the increasing need to be interactive with the world around us, we know that today's students will face significant challenges as they leave our schools. We know as well that in the late 1980s, the world of education had a choice to make: create graduates who could compete in a global context or create graduates who were aware of the world they lived in and were willing to make the changes to ensure sustainability. The former took precedence in curriculum and evaluation rubrics; however, that too is changing. Developing global consciousness is rapidly becoming a necessary skill amongst all students, at all levels. The timing of the appearance of *THINQ 4–6* in classrooms could not be better.

When the Canadian Education Association conducted the research "Teaching the Way We Aspire to Teach" a few years ago, we quickly realized that there were numerous examples across the country of teachers being successful in classrooms. An even deeper investigation into these classrooms demonstrated that tapping into the curiosity of students and formulating inquiry-based questions were amongst the key components. The teachers were able to generate high levels of intellectual engagement via the use of dynamic and innovative approaches into their classrooms. This is significant given how prescriptive curriculum and assessment currently are in our schools. Educators do know that measurement and use of data are important tools for improvement; however, ensuring that classrooms continue to be the centres of inquiry-investigation is the key to true success.

A compelling attribute of *THINQ 4–6* is that it targets the most critical stages of student life. Past and current research continues to illustrate that at this moment of a child's education (grades 4–6), these years are the true indicators of how well a student will do later in their schooling. This tool in classrooms will definitely serve teachers well, but more importantly, it presents additional resources in a format that is both stimulating and visually appealing. It challenges teachers to reflect further upon their instruction but in a manner that is supportive and appreciative.

During my conferences and workshops, I am frequently asked to present and describe the "21st Century Classroom." For some time, I was not able to clearly articulate that vision until I spent more time in classrooms and then it "hit" me. The "21st Century Classroom" is actually the current kindergarten classes in our schools. Amongst the many features that it has is the constant "feeding" of questions to children, some about their environment, some about their feelings, some about developing a skill and the need for it, but the one specific component that kindergarten classes have is an inquiry-based format. Sure, there is skills development but within this context, students are truly intellectually engaged via an inquiry-based approach. From the time that students leave that level of instruction, research demonstrates that their engagement levels decrease, becoming manifest in particular at the grades 4–6 levels, and continues to drop off as they enter high school. *THINQ 4–6* brings to the classroom an opportunity to replicate what happened a few years earlier and in a manner that is concise, pragmatic and not specific to one curriculum or another.

THINQ 4–6 also brings about opportunities for teachers to further their success stories in classrooms via the identification of challenges to change. Too often in education, we are "solutions-based," but don't take into account the same challenges that have prevented change from emerging in classrooms, schools or districts. I believe that *THINQ 4–6* asserts itself by asking some of the key questions that teachers need to ask, and also helps in finding the solutions. Trusting teachers more will definitely provide increases in student achievement and that can be attained via *THINQ 4–6*. This is more than just a resource. It can be a guide to further exploration of pedagogical approaches that serve to further promote imagination in classrooms. It can be a catalyst to bringing teachers together to map out strategies that generate increased student intellectual engagement.

In effect, *THINQ 4–6* will ensure that my 1976 classroom truly becomes a thing of the past, a distant memory that is no longer relevant in today's schools.

Ron Canuel
President and Chief Executive Officer
Canadian Education Association

ABOUT THE AUTHORS

photo Jill Colyer

Jill Colyer

Jill is currently the Director of Teaching and Learning at Bayview Glen Independent School. She was recently an Education Officer in the Curriculum and Assessment Policy Branch of the Ontario Ministry of Education and prior to that, the National Director of the Historical Thinking Project, a pan-Canadian educational initiative focused on the reform of history education. Jill was a secondary school teacher and department head with the Waterloo Region District School Board for 15 years, and has been a writer of curriculum materials, courses, textbooks, teaching guides and assessment tools throughout her career. Jill has had a long-term relationship as a writer and editor with the CBC. Jill acts as a consultant to educational publishers and gives workshops to teachers and administrators across the country. Her most recent publication is *IQ: A Practical Guide to Inquiry-based Learning*, Oxford University Press (2014).

photo Jennifer Watt

Jennifer Watt

Jennifer is an instructional leader for beginning teachers and their mentors at the Toronto District School Board. She has been a history, politics, social science and English teacher, and a consultant and coordinator for over 27 years. Throughout her career, she has supported both new and experienced classroom teachers at all grade levels and subject areas in thinking about how to share their knowledge, experience and practices to improve student learning and establish professional communities. Jennifer has a Master's Degree focusing on the assessment of teacher practice. She is the author of several books, as well as exemplars and curriculum units. Her most recent publication is *IQ: A Practical Guide to Inquiry-based Learning*, Oxford University Press (2014).

ACKNOWLEDGEMENTS

I would like to thank all of the teachers and administrators who have been willing to have frank conversations about the successes and challenges they face in their classrooms, schools and school systems. I continue to be impressed by the commitment and dedication educators have to their work, and their deep love for their students, despite the many pressures they face.

I am grateful for the love and support of my family and friends, and feel lucky to get to share my life with my husband David. Special thanks to my friend and writing partner Jennifer Watt, and to Tom Metuzals, who really is part of the circle of women.

Jill Colyer

Thanks to all those who said to me "I enjoyed your book." I probably didn't respond with adequate enthusiasm since I was somewhat embarrassed by your compliment. But I really, truly appreciate your support and your amazing efforts in inquiry learning.

To my husband Barry, you are amazing. To the rest of my family, Emma, Sean, Matt, Mom and Marion, you bring me joy. Thanks also to my brilliant writing partners, Jill and David.

Jennifer Watt

Advisory Panel

We would also like to thank the following educators who generously read chapters from the book and shared with us their comments and suggestions.

Camille Logan, Student Achievement Officer, Ontario Ministry of Education; Principal on Secondment, York Region District School Board

John Kershaw, Former Deputy Minister of Education (Anglophone), New Brunswick; Co-founder C21 Canada

Byron Stevenson, President, Ontario Elementary Social Studies Teachers' Association; Instructional Leader, Toronto District School Board

Keith Millions, Team Lead, French Language Services Branch, Alberta Education

Beverly McArthur, Instructional Coordinator, Peel District School Board

Dale Martelli, President, British Columbia Social Studies Teachers' Association; Flex Humanities Coordinator & Social Studies Department Head, Vancouver Technical Secondary School

About THINQ

Making inquiry-based learning a practical reality for every classroom!

An ever increasing number of educators are exploring the potential of inquiry-based pedagogies to build a bridge to teaching, learning and assessment in a digital age. They instinctively understand that asking questions and seeking answers is a natural way of being a learner in the world. However, translating this basic truth into daily instructional practice is no small thing. This is the focus of *THINQ* — to help make inquiry-based learning a practical reality for every classroom, teacher and student.

We are writing the *THINQ* professional learning series from a teacher perspective, with an empathetic and realistic appreciation of a teacher's daily challenges. *THINQ* is designed to help teachers see how, over time, they can realistically integrate more inquiry-based learning into the context of their own classrooms.

THINQ resources are designed to:

- encourage teachers to do more inquiry.
- explore the big ideas of inquiry in an accessible and reader-friendly way.
- make explicit what inquiry can look, feel and sound like.
- demonstrate how inquiry-based learning can be assessed and evaluated.
- pose deep questions for teacher self-reflection and discussion with colleagues.
- provide case studies that introduce practical strategies with contextual examples.
- address common teacher questions and misconceptions about inquiry.

THINQ emphasizes the big ideas that underpin inquiry-based learning regardless of grades and disciplines. We also apply them to the specific needs and characteristics of learners at different ages and developmental stages: *THINQ Kindergarten*, *THINQ 1–3* (Primary), *THINQ 4–6* (Junior) and *THINQ 7–9* (Intermediate). We recognize that school jurisdictions organize their schools and grade divisions differently, but all of us share the understanding that there are distinct developmental learning stages. So while "junior learner" may not be the designation for grades 4–6 in your system, we feel confident, based on our work with teachers, that the students, issues and challenges are the same.

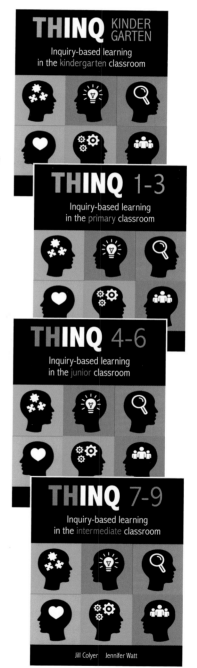

Professional learning — a personal journey

We believe that transforming the daily assessment and instructional practice of teachers is the single most important consideration in transitioning the traditional education system to digital-age teaching and learning models. But because change is hard, it is only really achievable if and when educators, individually and in collaborative communities, believe passionately in its benefits. They must choose voluntarily (not through coercion or compliance) to take up the challenge to change classroom practice and school culture. This is what *THINQ* is all about — helping educators reflect upon and move forward along their individual professional learning path.

We believe that integrating more inquiry rests, in part, upon a deep **conviction** that inquiry-based learning is needed and a personal **commitment** to persist until classrooms and schools begin to operate differently. Building the **capacity** to implement more inquiry in the **context** of one's own classroom and school is only sustainable if positive outcomes are **confirmed** by evidence and shared with others. Margin prompts throughout this book use these five Cs to provoke reflection, individually or with your colleagues, about your journey into inquiry-based learning.

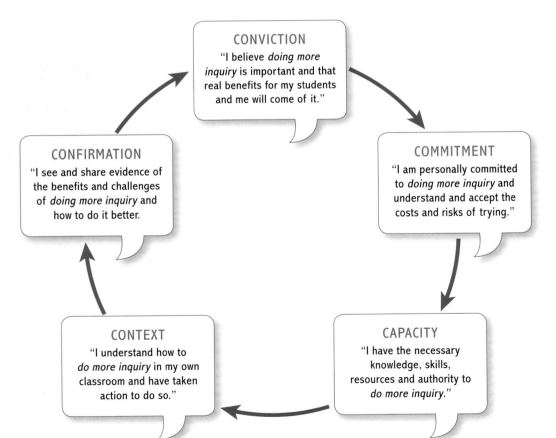

CONVICTION
"I believe *doing more inquiry* is important and that real benefits for my students and me will come of it."

COMMITMENT
"I am personally committed to *doing more inquiry* and understand and accept the costs and risks of trying."

CAPACITY
"I have the necessary knowledge, skills, resources and authority to *do more inquiry*."

CONTEXT
"I understand how to *do more inquiry* in my own classroom and have taken action to do so."

CONFIRMATION
"I see and share evidence of the benefits and challenges of *doing more inquiry* and how to do it better."

THINQ

- How well do these statements reflect where you and your colleagues are currently?

- What is the relationship between the Five Cs?

- How can you use the Five Cs to assess progress on your professional quest to do more inquiry?

Chapter 1
GETTING STARTED:
Inquiry-based learning with junior learners

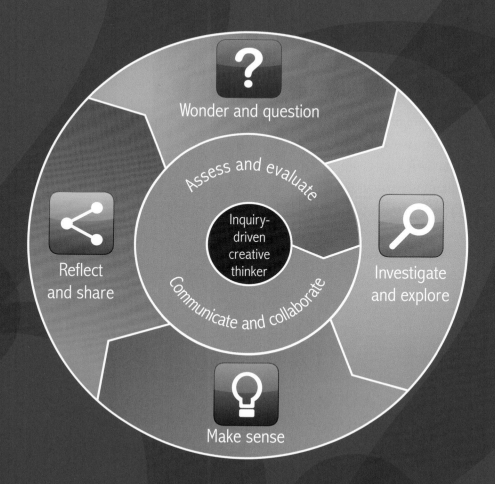

1.1 What is inquiry learning?

Inquiry learning is rooted in our curiosity and innate desire to make sense of the mysterious world. When we ask questions, determine a problem and use our heads and our hearts to investigate what fascinates us, we are engaged in inquiry.

Inquiry learning is not the latest educational fad, although it may seem to be due to its renewed popularity. It is not an innovation or a program. It is a way of being as a learner in the world and it is also a specific type of pedagogical practice. By pedagogical practice, we mean what you consider important for your students to learn and the purposeful steps you take to make that learning happen.

Inquiry learning has been around as long as teachers have encouraged and supported intellectual curiosity. Socrates is often cited as one of the first recorded inquiry teachers of antiquity. So why is the age-old practice of inquiry learning making a resurgence in education? Inquiry poses an alternative to rote learning. It is a form of deep learning that allows children to learn *how* to learn as opposed to making children learn *what* to learn in the form of isolated and fragmented content.

Teachers are no longer a main source of facts. The Internet houses more information than any learner could ever require or acquire. In a world where technology makes it easy to find answers and assists us in digging deeper into topics that fascinate us, education has a new purpose. That purpose is to foster curiosity and the asking of deeper questions, encouraging the use of intellect and conscience to answer these questions, and to provide opportunities to share new knowledge. Today, asking the right question is perhaps the most important step in finding the right answer.

THINQ

- How do the quotes of Wiesel, Dewey, hooks and Einstein support inquiry learning?
- How do these quotes resonate with you as a teacher and as a learner?
- What do you consider the essential traits of inquiry learning?
- Is it important to have a common understanding of what inquiry-based learning is at your school?

BIG IDEA

We learn by asking questions (inquiring).

FOOD FOR THOUGHT

"In the word question, there is a beautiful word — quest. I love that word."

Elie Wiesel

"Every thinker puts some portion of an apparently stable world in peril and no one can wholly predict what will emerge in its place."

John Dewey

"My hope emerges from those places of struggle where I witness individuals positively transforming their lives and the world around them. Educating is always a vocation rooted in hopefulness. As teachers we believe that learning is possible, that nothing can keep an open mind from seeking after knowledge and finding a way to know."

bell hooks

"It is, in fact, nothing short of a miracle that the modern methods of instruction have not yet entirely strangled the holy curiosity of inquiry; for this delicate little plant, aside from stimulation, stands mainly in need of freedom; without this it goes to wrack and ruin without fail. It is a grave mistake to think that the enjoyment of seeing and searching can be promoted by means of coercion and a sense of duty."

Albert Einstein

1.2 What are inquiry dispositions?

Curiosity, open-mindedness and confidence in your ability to reason are inquiry dispositions — or what some call "inquiry habits of mind." They are what keeps the learner on the journey of inquiry. These dispositions support risk-taking and commitment to inquiry learning. They make us perseverant and accepting of failure and mistakes as an important part of the journey.

Teachers should spend significant time creating an inquiry classroom culture that supports both the affective and the cognitive elements of inquiry learning. Students should expect a range of emotions while completing an inquiry — from joy and wonder to challenge and frustration. Checking in frequently with your students will help validate their emotions as well as provide information on how you can support their thinking and dispositions.

You can begin by modelling these dispositions to your students. What are you curious about? What makes you wonder? What questions have driven and continue to drive your life? Your students benefit from hearing your experiences as an inquiry learner and in seeing first hand your enthusiasm for aspects of life that they may or may not have considered.

At the heart of an inquiry community are learners who feel supported by each other. Getting to know your students, their identities, their cultures and their communities goes a long way in helping you build an inquiry community. The chart below offers some preliminary suggestions on how inquiry dispositions can flourish in your classroom.

BIG IDEA

Inquiry dispositions support risk-taking and a sustainable commitment to inquiry learning.

CONVICTION
How convinced are you that curiosity, criticality, hopefulness and open-mindedness are necessary conditions for learning?

COMMITMENT
When have you been most engaged as a learner and why?

Curiosity	**Criticality**	**Hopefulness**	**Open-mindedness**
Eagerness to learn or know something	Objective analysis and evaluation	Feeling or inspiring optimism about the future	Willingness to consider new ideas

FIGURE 1.1 Curiosity, criticality, hopefulness and open-mindedness are the essential building blocks for creating a sustainable culture of inquiry-based learning.

Disposition	Description	Ways to promote the disposition in your classroom
Curiosity and wonder	You see the world as mysterious and have many questions and interests as you try to make sense of the world.	Create and share simple, open-ended yet purposeful provocations with your students to invite, entice and expand intellectual curiosity on a specific topic or concept. Common provocations include an interesting photo, book, picture, natural object, question, event, or an interest of the students. Create a wonder wall of student questions. Share your own curiosities, pivotal questions, interests, and the successes and pitfalls of your own inquiry endeavours.
Criticality (critical thinking)	You enjoy thinking deeply. This thinking may involve making predictions, verifying evidence and assessing arguments and claims. You do not accept arguments based purely on authority (because someone else said so) You like to figure things out for yourself. You take risks in thinking and accept that mistakes and errors are essential for learning.	Teach students and provide students with opportunities to: • construct and recognize valid arguments and conclusions. • recognize common mistakes (fallacies) in reasoning. • distinguish between evidence and interpretation of evidence. • continually reinforce that learning to think deeply is a challenge for everyone and that learning involves making mistakes (highlight your own mistakes to students and how you learn from them).
Hopefulness	You see the world as it is and like to think how it can be improved. You do not accept the ways things are as inevitable. You care about and have a sense of purpose in your inquiries.	Inquiries involve problem-solving — they are future oriented. Do not deaden an inquiry process by presenting current knowledge as the be-all and end-all. Allow student to create their own knowledge and to be change agents. Recognize and model wonder about the world.
Open-mindedness	You are open to surprises. You consider many sides and perspectives when thinking. You are aware of your own biases and actively seek new questions and ideas about the world that you may not have considered before.	Highlight mysteries, big ideas and questions about the world. In preparing guided inquiries, be sure to provide evidence and arguments from multiple perspectives for students to consider. Provide multiple opportunities for students to self-reflect on their thinking. Tempt students out of their comfort zone by providing opportunities for them to learn more about themselves, their communities and the world. Have students create an "amazing and astonishing" wall that highlights new learning they have discovered through the inquiry process.

FIGURE 1.2 There are many ways to promote inquiry dispositions in your classroom.

Am I already doing inquiry learning?

Teachers frequently ask us for reassurance ("Am I doing inquiry?") since they employ a wide variety of instructional strategies or research methods in their classrooms. These teachers may already be extremely proficient in encouraging inquiry disposition such as curiosity and critical thinking in their students.

It has been our experience that the vast majority of teachers are engaged in some type of inquiry learning and many are doing considerable amounts of inquiry throughout the school day.

If you are asking students open-ended questions, if you are provoking their curiosity and if you are supporting them to think deeply about their own learning and the world around them, you are "doing inquiry."

So the issue for most teachers is not if they are "doing inquiry," the real issue is how we can get better; better by offering more opportunities for inquiry, by deepening opportunities for thinking at each stage of inquiry, by clarifying our own understanding of inquiry skills and dispositions and by broadening our practices of the assessment of inquiry. And that's where this book comes in. We hope to offer practical support in deepening and supporting you and your students' inquiry work.

CONTEXT
How much inquiry are you currently doing in your classroom?

CAPACITY
What do you think you need to learn in order to do more and better inquiry?

THINQ

- How do you build a classroom culture that supports inquiry dispositions?
- How do you see yourself reflected in these inquiry dispositions?
- How could your school be more reflective of these inquiry dispositions?

1.3 I say inquiry, you say inquiry: Are we talking about the same thing?

BIG IDEA

All knowledge is living and changing because it is personally and socially constructed.

We have found the term "inquiry" to be an elusive term since inquiry learning shares important purposes and traits of other pedagogies such as constructivist learning, active learning, discovery learning, student-centered learning, collaborative learning, 21st century learning, transformational learning, critical pedagogies and others. To simplify, all these pedagogies share a purpose, and that purpose is to make a child an effective and independent learner by giving them opportunities to build knowledge.

CONFIRMATION

In your experience, do children learn best when they are actively involved in "building knowledge"? Why or why not?

For all of these pedagogies, knowledge is living and changing because it is socially and personally constructed. Students learn best when they are invited to be part of the active and exciting process of knowledge building. Learners are no longer viewed as containers to be filled with disconnected bits of knowledge; they are naturally curious, rational and committed to making sense of their world.

Teachers also should be intellectually engaged in their craft and not merely following lock-step curricular or instructional mandates. Teachers are not all-knowing authority figures but are skilled facilitators and talented conceptual thinkers who can provoke wonder in their students. So when teachers grapple in trying to distinguish inquiry from other pedagogies, it is helpful to remember what these have in common — an inquiry orientation in how knowledge is created, built and shared.

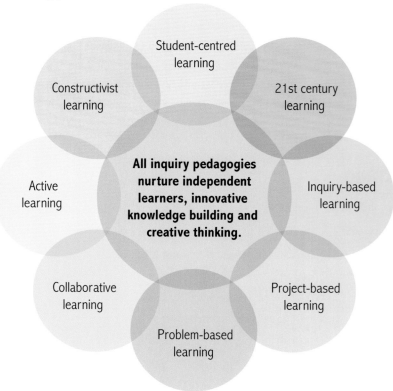

FIGURE 1.3 All inquiry-type pedagogies share a common purpose.

Student-centred learning

Constructivist learning

21st century learning

Active learning

All inquiry pedagogies nurture independent learners, innovative knowledge building and creative thinking.

Inquiry-based learning

Collaborative learning

Project-based learning

Problem-based learning

1.4 Isn't there a standard type of inquiry or method of inquiry?

In addition to pedagogies that include inquiry purposes and qualities, there are also discrete types of inquiry for teachers to choose from. These include problem-based learning, project-based learning, play-based learning and design-based instruction, to name just a few. Your grade division or school or school district may be trying out various forms of inquiry-based learning, or is a proponent of one or two in particular.

It is easy to become overwhelmed with so many choices of inquiry learning. Some inquiry types focus on technology, especially in the sharing of new ideas with a larger world audience. Some deal more with the creation and innovation of objects while others remain more in the realm of ideas. Some types are aimed at different age groups. Nonetheless, what we find helpful is to grasp the three essential traits of all types of inquiry learning.

Essential traits of inquiry

1. Inquiry is rooted in an essential question that invites the learner to wonder, think deeply and solve.

2. Answering the question or solving the problem involves a method. This method involves discrete steps or stages of a cycle that help the learner with their thinking. This method may be particular to a discipline.

3. In answering the question or solving the problem, the student experiences a developmentally appropriate version of the way professional or expert learners in a field engage in their work. Like professionals, they think critically, self-reflect, contribute, communicate and share findings. New knowledge is created.

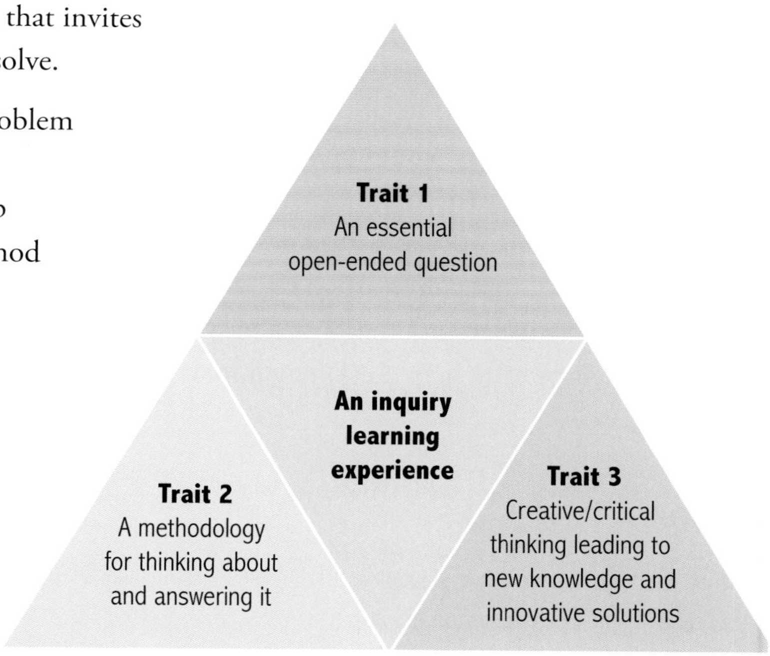

> **BIG IDEA**
> All inquiry learning, regardless of grade or discipline, has three common essential traits.

> **CAPACITY**
> Do you feel you have a clear understanding of the nature of inquiry learning? What else would you like to know?

Trait 1
An essential open-ended question

An inquiry learning experience

Trait 2
A methodology for thinking about and answering it

Trait 3
Creative/critical thinking leading to new knowledge and innovative solutions

FIGURE 1.4 All inquiry learning experiences share three essential traits.

Discipline-based inquiry models

In addition to the many types and variations of inquiry, there exists yet another factor that distinguishes inquiry. Each discipline has its own way of building knowledge and verifying what it considers quality work. The process of inquiry learning tends to reflect the particular qualities of the specific disciplines of the inquiry. If you are doing a math inquiry or a historical inquiry or a visual arts inquiry, the method, stages, processes and questions of the inquiry can be distinct.

Consider the five visual models of inquiry processes on the following page. These visual models are helpful in supporting the understanding of teachers and students since they are an attempt to represent the complexity involved in the inquiry process. Referring to the models frequently and consistently helps teachers and students address concerns and provide appropriate instructional support.

Don't be deceived by some of the linear ways in which inquiry can be represented. Experienced inquirers know that the process is responsive to the individual, recursive, non-linear and flexible, with a lot of "looping back" unlike more traditional models of a research process.

These are just five examples of inquiry processes based on a particular discipline. Your curriculum documents may outline specific inquiry processes that you and your students should be using. Does this mean you have to become experts in all the disciplinary methods of inquiry? Certainly not, but it does help to recognize that there are differences to consider. We advise avoiding getting bogged down in the many distinctions, especially when you are working with junior learners. We recommend instead that you focus on the three shared essential traits and purposes. Discipline and interdisciplinary examples are provided in upcoming chapters to help clarify any important differences in inquiry processes.

How inquiry models can help

Inquiry models:

- represent a holistic view of active knowledge creation.

- attempt to simplify complex learning experiences.

- use "steps" to highlight important distinctions in thinking.

- facilitate thinking important to the discipline.

- focus on process of knowledge creation rather than outcome.

- remind learners to pause, stop and think as thinking proceeds and deepens.

- highlight transferable skills.

- stress collaboration at all stages in order to make meaning.

- vary in usefulness according to context.

FIGURE 1.5 Inquiry models can be helpful to learning in many different ways.

THINQ

- What are the differences and similarities between the various inquiry processes represented in the graphics on the next page?

- Why may it be important for your students to use different inquiry processes?

- What other inquiry processes are you familiar with?

- Which ones do you think are most helpful to your learners and why?

FIGURE 1.6 A scientific inquiry model focuses on experimentation and discovery (C. Bruner, 2014).

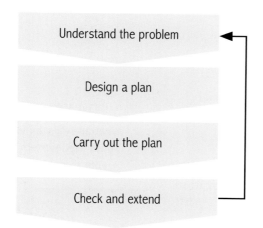

FIGURE 1.7 Polya's mathematical inquiry model focuses on solving problems.

FIGURE 1.8 Design-and-build inquiry focuses on innovation and doing and making things better.

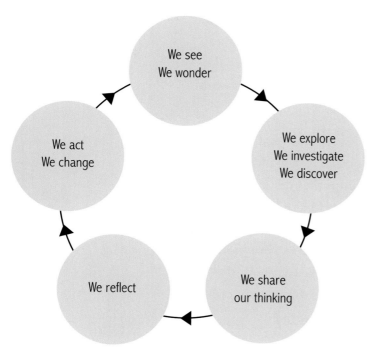

FIGURE 1.9 A social studies inquiry focuses on wondering about, exploring and understanding the world.

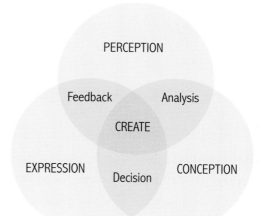

FIGURE 1.10 An arts inquiry or creative process model is focused on the act of creation.

1.5 Why is inquiry a better way to learn?

So this is where we come in, educators who believe that inquiry learning promises a "better way to learn." But how is it a better way to learn? Let's consider some fundamental beliefs about learners and then turn to recent educational research that supports the belief that inquiry is a good way to learn.

Beliefs about learners

Inquiry learning is rooted in progressive and constructivist educational philosophies of the early 19th century. Progressive educators, such as John Dewey, proposed that learners should "do" the discipline by thinking, communicating and verifying knowledge in an authentic manner. He felt passive transmission-based pedagogies were flawed since the memorization of facts, discreet procedures and algorithms were quickly forgotten because the learner had no part in working with them or in building new knowledge that was relevant to them or to the real world.

Paulo Freire's critical pedagogy labelled education a "banking model" with the teacher filling the learner's mind with information. Learners were passive and oppressed by an education that was imposed on them. He advocated for an education where learners would critically engage with knowledge, where they would grapple and build upon what is known, and strive to change the world based on this new knowledge.

Central to inquiry learning are beliefs in who learners are and what they are capable of. Inquiry learning encourages human curiosity. It demands rational thought. It is grounded in what is already known but pushes the learner to add to this knowledge through a process in which they explore the ideas again from new perspectives and viewpoints. Learners are in control. They are active participants, not passive recipients. Learning is a collaborative endeavour. Ideally, learners should be self-motivated, confident and excited about the inquiry. Inquiry learning deals with "real world" problems that are important to our students, who they are, and what is important to them.

Inquiry learning can be a transformational mode of learning. It changes the learner and the learning community, both in and beyond the classroom walls.

Research about inquiry learning

Scientific research on learning supports the theoretical claims of these respected education theorists. Dr. Sharon Friesen and David Scott (*Inquiry-Based Learning: A Review of the Research Literature*, 2013) thoughtfully detail a diverse and wide body of research on the most common types of inquiry learning in North America. Some of the highlights of their research suggest:

- inquiry-based approaches to learning positively impact students' ability to understand core concepts and procedures. Inquiry also creates a more engaging learning environment.

- disciplinary-based inquiry does not detract from traditional forms of assessment but actually increases achievement on traditional forms of standardized assessment (Friesen, 2010).

- discipline-based approaches to inquiry learning (as opposed to minimally-guided instruction), if designed well, support students in deep learning.

- inquiry helps students develop their critical thinking abilities and scientific reasoning, while developing a deeper understanding of science (Barrow, 2006).

- problem-based learning increases student engagement in mathematics, leads to less anxiety towards mathematics, a greater willingness to see mathematics as relevant to everyday life, and increases willingness to approach mathematical challenges with a positive attitude (Boaler, 1997).

- problem-based learning fosters greater gains in conceptual understanding in science (Williams, Hemstreet, Liu and Smith, 1998).

> **CONVICTION**
> How convinced are you that research provides evidence of the benefits of inquiry learning? What else would you like to see?

> **CONFIRMATION**
> Do your own classroom experiences confirm or contradict the research?

Benefits of inquiry-based learning
More engaging learning environments
Positive impact on student core conceptual understanding
Increased student achievement (even on standardized tests)
Fosters critical, creative, innovative thinking
Greater student engagement
Improved student attitudes to learning

FIGURE 1.11 Research indicates there are significant benefits to taking an inquiry stance to learning.

Inquiry-based learning in the Information Age

Inquiry-based learning takes on a whole new dimension for students living in the Information Age. Teachers and textbooks are no longer the only expert sources of knowledge. When motivated, students can access a multiverse of sources and information to satisfy their curiosity. More powerfully still, this inquiry process can be personalized to meet each students' interests and learning preferences. Students are no longer limited to traditional one-size-fits-all tools and processes for gathering sources.

It's imperative, however, that students hone their analytical skills when faced with so much information from so many sources; that they become critical consumers and responsible creators of information. Teachers can respond to this need by modelling and facilitating the kind of analytical thinking required to conduct inquiry. They might also expect that the process and products of learning will not look the same as they once did.

It is reasonable to expect that teachers will respond to students' considerable skill with digital technologies by encouraging their thoughtful, purposeful and creative use — whether by encouraging Internet searches for evidence; collaborating on solving problems in a social network; or sharing ideas, conclusions and questions with the wider digital world.

FIGURE 1.12 By taking an inquiry stance, many important aspects of best-practice teaching, learning and assessment can be addressed.

THINQ BIG

Inquiry learning: A bridge to the future

As our world continues to change at an ever increasing rate, reforming and transforming education to teaching and learning in a digital age can seem a daunting task. In our view, inquiry-based learning represents an overarching big idea that offers a possible bridge to the future.

In the same way, the goal of putting a person on the moon offered a powerful vision that engaged millions of people around the world. Achieving this goal was immensely complicated, involving thousands of people doing things that had never been done before. All of this activity and complexity was glued together by a single central vision.

Inquiry-based learning offers similar possibilities for education. In taking an inquiry stance, the challenges of 21st century learning can be tackled, not by focusing on dozens of different priorities, but on a singular, powerful and overarching vision of inquiry that can be shared across schools, disciplines and grades.

Traditional learning	Inquiry learning
Have to learn	Want to learn
What to know	How to know
Tell and memorize	Ask and inquire
Only one right answer	Many possible conclusions
Teacher directed	Learner centered
One-size-fits-all	Personalized
Passive learning	Active learning
Assessment for marks	Assessment for learning

1.6 What is the junior teacher's role in inquiry learning?

When we talk with junior teachers who use inquiry learning, we learn a lot from them and about them. Firstly, these teachers believe that they are learning alongside their students and are excited by the prospect of doing so. They are passionate and curious about their disciplines and about critical and creative thought.

They "think big" by identifying essential concepts and skills and they don't abandon those big ideas, even when faced with pressures of coverage, standardized tests and other external mandates. They have confidence in their students' abilities and are responsive to their interests. These teachers take appropriate risks in their teaching by challenging students to think deeper, to question, to refute, to support, to interrogate, to consider many perspectives, and to stretch beyond the obvious and easy-to-answer questions.

These teachers talk about overcoming their own fear and trepidation when conducting an inquiry due to the reality that they never know for sure what may happen. This initial fear changes to excitement over time and in seeing the benefits to student learning and engagement. These teachers have tried and stumbled and tried again to create and hone strategies to make their students better inquiry learners.

> **BIG IDEA**
> Inquiry learning is a continuum, with guided inquiry and a large degree of teacher direction at one end, and open inquiry with a large degree of student autonomy at the other.

> **COMMITMENT**
> How comfortable are you with the possibility of changing your role as a teacher?

Traditional teaching	Inquiry teaching
Teacher is the expert	Teacher **is a co-learner**
Teacher tells	Teacher **models**
Teacher controls	Teacher **activates**
Teacher corrects mistakes	Teacher **gives feedback**
Teacher gives answers	Teacher **asks questions**
Teacher is a manager	Teacher **is a mentor**
Teacher assesses task completion	Teacher **assesses learning**

FIGURE 1.13 In an inquiry learning classroom, students benefit when teachers participate as co-learners who model and activate learning.

From guided to open inquiry

Some of the nervousness many teachers feel when planning inquiry learning is due to a misconception involving the appropriate degree of student autonomy. Inquiry learning is a continuum that begins with a large degree of teacher direction and a small degree of student autonomy. The continuum extends to the point of no teacher direction and complete student autonomy; this is called "open inquiry." The latter is more of an idealized horizon on the continuum of guided inquiry.

You know your learners best. A learner who has little experience with asking questions, selecting and assessing evidence and drawing conclusions needs direct instruction and modelling. Not providing that instruction, modeling and the opportunity to practice would only frustrate that learner.

Sometimes the learner is good at asking questions and gathering evidence, but is not very skilled at synthesis, evaluation or critical self-reflection. This student doesn't need the teacher to model scaffolded questioning or evidence gathering, but they do need help to make them more self-directed in other aspects of critical thinking.

Rarely is there an inquiry experience in classrooms at either end of the continuum. Most inquiry learning is a blended version of teacher direction and student autonomy. Teachers, through careful consideration and using their knowledge of their students, explicitly plan, teach and model the stages of inquiry so that student proficiency increases and future inquiry opportunities can become increasingly student-directed. This, of course, is the ultimate goal of inquiry: giving students the power to conduct their own inquiries throughout their lives, independent of teachers and schooling.

WORDS MATTER

Guided
Conducted by a guide.

Open
Willing to consider many different possibilities.

Facilitate
To help something operate more smoothly and effectively.

Model
An example to copy.

Feedback
Information that is used as the basis for improvement.

CAPACITY
In your classroom, where would you place the readiness of you and your students on the continuum of guided to open inquiry?

HIGH
Teacher direction

HIGH
Student autonomy

Guided inquiry   **Blended inquiry**   **Open inquiry**

FIGURE 1.14
As you move from guided inquiry towards open inquiry, teacher direction decreases and student autonomy increases.

Another common misconception of inquiry is that it is the best or only teaching strategy that should be used in the classroom. Debates about the "best teaching strategy" are largely counterproductive in our view. In order for inquiry pedagogy to be successful, other strategies that promote learning, such as direct instruction, telling stories, practicing and mastering literacy, numeracy and performance skills, are also required.

Critics of inquiry learning (yes, they exist) claim that student learning is compromised when students are left to "discover" facts, procedures and skills without any assistance from a teacher. We can see their point. Students can become frustrated if asked to complete a cognitively demanding task with no prior experience or supporting knowledge. A considerable body of educational research shows that guided inquiry is the most effective form of inquiry learning.

COMMITMENT
Do any of these myths and misconceptions limit commitment to inquiry learning in your school?

FIGURE 1.15 There are many myths and misconceptions about what inquiry is and how it works.

Inquiry myths and misconceptions	Response
The teacher has no control.	Students do not conduct inquiry unassisted. In order to maximize the impact of an inquiry, teachers adopt powerful questioning strategies, scaffold the inquiry method so that students understand what they are doing and why they are doing it, and provide frequent formative feedback.
	If a teacher is not used to the active learning that occurs during an inquiry, they may view it as chaotic when in fact it is productive learning.
It takes too long.	An entire inquiry method or cycle does not have to be completed for important learning to happen. Teachers can focus on one or two aspects of an inquiry method. Inquiry can take more time than passive transmission models, but the resulting learning is deeper, more beneficial for the learner, and will address a number of overall expectations, big ideas, or essential understandings of subjects.
It's too hard for junior students.	To claim that students must have acquired or memorized a certain set of facts or have mastered a set of skills before they can conduct an inquiry is to deny them the opportunity to become active learners and deep thinkers. Likewise, claiming that students have to be of a certain age or language proficiency to conduct an inquiry is misguided.
It's difficult to assess.	Effective inquiry learning, like other learning strategies, is most effective when supported by formative assessment strategies. Teachers do not have to learn a host of new assessment and evaluation methods when engaged in inquiry-based learning; they can apply good fundamental principles of assessment as, for, and of learning to inquiry.
It's the best teaching strategy.	Inquiry learning benefits the learner in many ways. It is not the only way to learn, nor is it the most expedient way to learn in some instances (e.g., learning how to measure angles, blending colours for painting, how to work best in a collaborative group). Inquiry is best used to actively explore deep questions based on important curricular concepts. It is best balanced with other teaching strategies.

We have seen effective inquiry in action: at different grade levels, within different subject-based disciplines, and in vastly different settings (e.g., urban and rural schools, small and large schools). In this book, we aim to provide you with the practical advice and examples of inquiry learning that will act, not as a recipe for success, but a guide to deepen the inquiry learning that is already happening in your classroom. One feature this book offers is a number of instructive case studies.

In the following case study, begin by considering if the teacher is conducting an inquiry based on the three essential traits: (1) an essential open-ended question; (2) a method for thinking about and answering it; and (3) critical thinking, reflection and sharing, leading to the creation of new knowledge.

INQUIRY IN ACTION

Science: Is this inquiry?

Let's consider a snapshot of Emma's class with the question "Is it an inquiry?" in mind.

Emma's grade 4 class is studying the topic of the habitats and animals of North America and she would like to include more inquiry learning in this unit. She decides to let the students choose their own animal to research. Emma has provided visual organizers for the students to use to organize their research. Students are expected to present their findings to the class in a format of their choice, such as a diorama, a series of pictures with text or a poster.

Emma's plan has a good degree of student choice, which can increase student engagement. To be a true inquiry, however, Emma should be posing a deep inquiry question to guide the students' understanding of the concept of habitat — a question that allows factual information about any living thing to be added to the more important conceptual understanding. An example might be "How is habitat essential to an animal's survival?" or "Why should we protect habitats?" Inquiry is grounded in an open-ended question or problem. (Learning that is focused on closed-ended questions or problems are more accurately called research or calculations.)

Students would engage in further questioning to guide their gathering of sources. Maybe these questions would be posted on a "wonder wall" for that unit. Students could choose the "best" five questions for research on the animal's habitat (e.g., "What does this animal need to survive?" "What physical qualities of the animal reflect its habitat?" "Is this animal threatened because its habitat is changing?" "How do humans impact this habitat?").

They might also be engaged in the critical thinking demanded of an inquiry by assessing the sources of their research (e.g., "What sources are reliable?") by summarizing and synthesizing their research by using visual organizers provided by the teacher, and by drawing a viable conclusion based on the research.

Time is given throughout the inquiry for the students' critical reflection (e.g., "Is this the right question?" "Are these the best sources?" "Is there another way of thinking about this?" "Am I ready to make a conclusion?").

THINQ

- How else could Emma deepen or focus this learning to make it more authentic inquiry learning?

- Consider a learning activity that you do with your students that involves inquiry. How could you hone this activity to honour and deepen each stage of inquiry?

1.7 Are inquiry-based learning and the junior learner a good fit?

Inquiry learning is a good fit for the junior learner. Junior learners have emerging qualities that can be intentionally strengthened by inquiry learning experiences. The junior learner also faces unique challenges that an inquiry-focused classroom can address.

Characteristics of junior learners

In terms of emerging qualities, the junior learner is more intellectually and socially curious than a younger student. A classroom focus on collaborative wondering and questioning meets this junior learner's need.

The junior learner has more lived experiences and critical thinking capabilities to inform their learning. They benefit from investigating more complex topics that have no easy answers and that demand logic and reasoning. Junior learners also enjoy opportunities to test their thinking abilities.

They are more empathetic and have a more flexible sense of what is right and wrong compared with younger students. This ability to think with nuance, open-mindedness and to withhold judgment allows the junior learner to delve into open-ended inquiry questions without the same degree of frustration they may have felt at an earlier age.

Strengths of junior learners

Inquiry learning taps into the inherent strengths of the junior learner. Junior learners are at an age where they are beginning to critically examine the world. They notice that "things aren't always what they appear to be." Inconsistencies, contradictions and unfairness bother them and make them wonder about how things got this way and how to make them better. They are developing more sophistication as speakers, writers and listeners for a purpose. They tend to enjoy puzzles, mysteries and surprises in their thinking.

BIG IDEA

Inquiry learning taps into the inherent strengths of the junior learner.

Characteristics of junior learners

Junior learners ARE...

- intellectually and socially curious.
- empathetic and open-minded.
- aware of and bothered by unfairness and inconsistency.
- becoming less egocentric and more willing to collaborate with peers.
- increasingly autonomous of adults and less likely to accept arguments based on authority.
- vulnerable to embarrassment and loss of self-confidence when compared to others.

Junior learners CAN...

- investigate more complex questions with no easy answers.
- think with more nuance and withhold judgment.
- examine the world more critically and see that things aren't always as they appear.
- make more connections from their lives to the rest of the world.
- better sustain their interest and effort when learning is challenging.
- face new anxieties about real world problems and issues.

FIGURE 1.16 Inquiry-based learning offers junior learners many opportunities to express who they are and what they can do.

Their combined curiosity and energy help to sustain their interest even when learning becomes difficult. In a classroom that honours their voices and lived experiences as valuable, students make strong connections from their personal lives to the real world. They can gain confidence and determination to stay committed to learning, despite the challenges. They may like to wrestle with ideas together with their friends and fellow students. They develop beyond ego-centric concerns to a greater understanding of other people and communities.

Junior learners are more autonomous than younger children and feel the need to move away from adults towards peers. They may feel the need to challenge the adult world and to test boundaries. They realize that their beliefs may differ from others. The inquiry disposition of not accepting arguments purely on authority (because someone else said so) and wanting to figure things out for oneself mirrors the cognitive and social development of the junior learner.

As their sense of self builds, junior learners can feel vulnerable to embarrassment and may suffer a loss of self-confidence when compared to others. This trait creates challenges to traditional classroom assessment but not to the culture of learning required in an inquiry classroom. It's important to build a classroom culture that supports the inquiry dispositions of criticality and open-mindedness. By making sense of the world together, inquiry learning invites junior learners to take risks, contribute and share findings.

Junior learners can face new anxieties. They are moving away from fears of strangers, monsters and ghosts to real fears of wars, social injustices and environmental crisis. The junior learner realizes that actions in the present will impact the future, thus validating their fears. We have noted that one important inquiry

INQUIRY FOR ALL

Questions of personal significance

By focusing on asking questions and solving problems of personal significance, inquiry learning offers great potential to meet the needs of exceptional students. Tap into what students love to learn, regardless of whether it seems like a good curriculum fit. The student with passionate interests already brings prior knowledge that will assist them immensely throughout the inquiry process. Working collaboratively with peers in inquiry learning allows exceptional students to make friends, actively contribute and observe knowledge-building in action.

Students with special needs may require more support in the questioning and exploration part of an inquiry to gain the confidence needed to attempt new learning. These students will experience meaningful inquiry learning when teachers plan to focus on one or two appropriate inquiry skills (e.g., asking questions, recognizing reasons, developing reasons or sharing reasons) and allowing additional practice through questions of personal significance. Teachers should work together in a professional learning network to scaffold inquiry skills for exceptional students, perhaps through joint planning opportunities.

Teachers should communicate with the parents of exceptional students. One or two specific inquiry skills will assist students in making connections in their daily lives and helps to build and deepen these new inquiry skills. These skills may include social skills (e.g., taking turns in a group, giving positive feedback) and cognitive skills (e.g., using inquiry vocabulary, identifying reasons).

Teachers should always focus on the growth of the student in inquiry learning and celebrate and share these successes with the learner, peers and families.

disposition is the ability to be hopeful. Inquiry learning allows students to both create their own knowledge and to be change agents. Hopeful inquiry learners do not accept the ways things are as inevitable. Thus, inquiry learning can help to alleviate some of these anxieties.

Inquiry learning and junior learners are a good fit. This rapid development of thinking and socio-emotional abilities is an ideal time for inquiry learning.

Helping students to understand inquiry

It is helpful for students to understand what inquiry learning is. Here are three ways you can help students understand the process of inquiry:

- Have them define what it means to be an inquiry learner and to think about themselves as inquiry learners (see Reproducibles 1A, 1B and 1C). These reproducibles could be used as exit cards, learning or response journal entries, or as partnered sharing questions.

- Have them identify examples of powerful inquiries and people involved in them. Students can more fully appreciate the necessity of failure and making mistakes through the process when they see how other respected thinkers struggled before changing the world with their thinking.

- Post a visual of the inquiry method most suited to your students and the inquiry and refer to it frequently for the purpose of self-reflection (see Reproducible 1D).

FIGURES 1.17–1.20
Reproducibles 1A (p. RE1), 1B (p. RE2), 1C (p. RE3) and 1D (p. RE4).

Revisit and reflect

This introductory chapter explored the possibilities of inquiry learning, namely what it is, how it benefits the learner and the idea that inquiry is an age-old process of creating and building knowledge that remains dynamic and responsive to today's challenge of fostering inquiry-driven and creative thinkers. In the next chapter, we delve into the assessment of inquiry and how teachers can best support students as they learn through inquiry.

THINQ

- What are the opportunities and challenges for you in "going deeper" with inquiry learning?

- How do you or can you inspire your students to be creative and innovative in addressing challenges that arise during their inquiries?

- Which inquiry dispositions do your students possess? How might you model and support the growth of inquiry dispositions for your students?

- Consider Reproducible 1E, *Teacher self-assessment: Which pattern of inquiry best describes your practice?*

- Consider Reproducible 1F, *Teacher self-assessment: Inquiry readiness checklist.* How ready are you?

BIG IDEAS

1.1 We learn by asking questions (inquiring).

1.2 Inquiry dispositions support risk-taking and a sustainable commitment to inquiry learning.

1.3 All knowledge is living and changing because it is personally and socially constructed.

1.4 All inquiry learning, regardless of grade or discipline, has three common essential traits.

1.5 Central to inquiry learning are beliefs about who learners are and what they are capable of.

1.6 Inquiry learning is a continuum with guided inquiry and a large degree of teacher direction at one end, and open inquiry with a large degree of student autonomy at the other.

1.7 Inquiry learning taps into the inherent strengths of the junior learner.

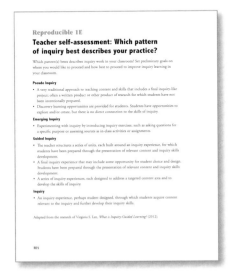

FIGURE 1.21 Reproducible 1E, p. RE5.

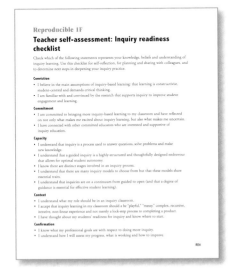

FIGURE 1.22 Reproducible 1F, p. RE6.

Chapter 2
ASSESSING AND EVALUATING:
Considering how our junior learners are doing

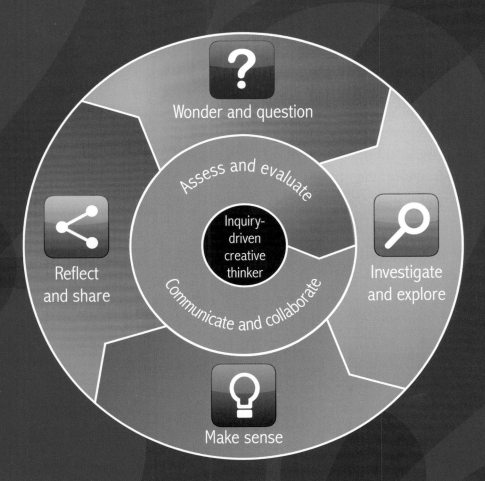

2.1 What is inquiry assessment?

Assessment, in a fundamental way, is about teachers and students pausing to reflect independently on the question, "How am I doing?" and collectively, "How are we doing?"

These questions relate to both academic and social-emotional learning. They allow us to consider our aims as individual learners and as a supportive learning community. They should empower and improve learning.

These fundamental questions can be revised to be more focused and specific to the inquiry activities and workings of your classroom. But the heart of assessment is teachers and students asking and answering these questions frequently.

Six essential abilities of inquiry learners

We consider this list of six essential abilities to be the core of inquiry activities and inquiry assessment. Inquiry topics and tasks can and should be as varied as each unique classroom and learner, but the six essential inquiry abilities remain the constant in inquiry assessment. This list of six helps you and your students know what is at the crux of inquiry. It can help you in common guided inquiry learning experiences for an entire class or for more independent inquiry experiences for individual students.

The first essential ability of an inquiry learner is to ask questions. Student proficiency and growth in this ability supports all the other essential abilities. For example, when we "think together," we ask questions of each other to clarify meaning, stretch thinking, uncover beliefs, and to offer another perspective, innovate or create something new. When we "understand

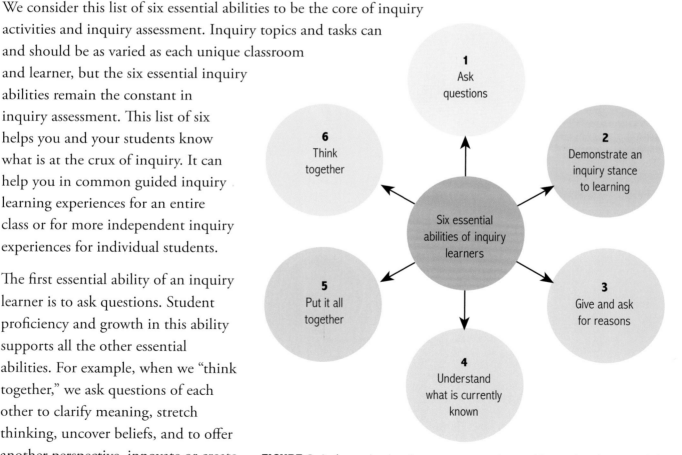

FIGURE 2.1 Assessing inquiry means assessing and improving the essential abilities of students as inquiry learners.

what is currently known," we also use our questioning skills to determine the credibility, point of view and authority of the information. Chapter 3, *Wondering and questioning* provides more detail on questioning and assessing this essential inquiry ability.

Keep in mind that the second essential inquiry ability is to foster inquiry dispositions. We provide a list of what we think are important inquiry dispositions in Chapter 1, *Getting started*. You should select the inquiry dispositions that have genuine meaning for your students and that reflect your particular school, district or ministry priorities. Many of these inquiry dispositions are reflected in learning skills and curricular expectations.

That being said, we feel that inquiry dispositions may get short-changed in classrooms and overlooked in assessment, often because these dispositions are not part of curriculum standards. This is wrong. Inquiry learning involves the whole child. It is social learning; not just the acquisition of isolated skills or information. So our belief is that inquiry dispositions influence students' abilities to be playful, creative and strong thinkers. Inquiry dispositions contribute to the formation of a child's individual identity and their future potential in a complex, knowledge rich and knowledge-driven world.

It is especially important for students to have time to reflect on their inquiry dispositions while in the process of an inquiry, and not just at the end. Reproducible 2A, *How to model and assess inquiry dispositions* defines the dispositions, suggests what they look like in the classroom, outlines how inquiry learning supports the disposition and provides a set of questions that students could use as self-assessment.

The third essential inquiry ability, to give and ask for reasons, applies to high level critical thinking processes such as synthesizing, predicting, assessing and evaluating. You may want to make this ability, or any of the others, more specific for a particular unit.

The fourth essential inquiry ability relates to a student's understanding of content knowledge. Chapter 4, *Investigating and exploring* provides more detail on assessing the essential inquiry ability of understanding what is known.

The fifth ability is one of application, and drawing and communicating conclusions. Chapter 5, *Making sense* provides more detail on assessing the essential inquiry ability of putting it all together.

> ## CAPACITY
> How do you feel about your capacity to identify and assess the essential inquiry abilities of your students? What else do you need to know or do?

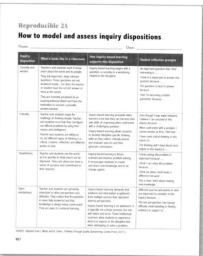

FIGURE 2.2 Reproducible 2A, p. RE7.

The sixth ability, thinking together, asks students to listen to each other with respect; to build on each other's ideas; to assist each other in drawing inferences from what has been said, read or observed; and to seek to identify one another's assumptions and beliefs. These "reasoning together" abilities were articulated in Matthew Lipman's model of student-led "communities of inquiry" detailed in his work from the 1970s. Lipman's community of inquiry grew from his belief in Dewey's work on promoting greater democracy in education. Lipman's model demanded that students both think for themselves (critical skills) and think cooperatively (dialogic skills). Chapter 6, *Reflecting and sharing*, provides more detail on the essential inquiry ability of thinking together.

If you think that these six abilities are a workable place to start your inquiry assessment planning, you need, firstly, to detail what excellence might look like in each of these abilities and secondly, to create possible learning activities that will allow you to gather varied and rich assessment evidence. Reproducible 2B, *The six essential inquiry abilities for assessment* may assist you in your initial planning.

Students benefit from multiple opportunities to discuss the question "Who is an inquiry learner?" by examining real-life examples of inquiry learners from their communities. Reproducible 2C, *Student exploration: Who is an inquiry learner?* may serve as a starting point for students to define, in their own words, the abilities of inquiry learners.

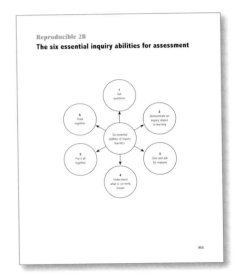

FIGURE 2.3 Reproducible 2B, p. RE8.

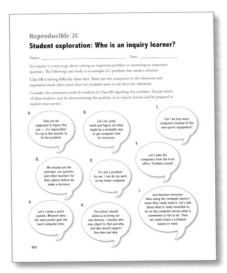

FIGURE 2.4 Reproducible 2C, p. RE9.

THINQ

- How could the six essential abilities of an inquiry learner help both teachers and students understand what is the crux of inquiry learning?

- How could you use the six essential abilities of an inquiry learner to assist in planning formative and summative assessments?

- How do the six essential abilities converge and support your mandated curriculum?

- How could your students self-assess their own learning goals in relation to the six essential abilities?

2.2 How do I assess what's essential to inquiry along with everything else?

As controversial as this may seem, we feel it is virtually impossible to "cover" in any deep, meaningful and beneficial way through learning and assessment activities, all the content and skills prescribed in even the most progressive of curriculum documents and state standards.

As teachers, we may run ourselves ragged trying to figure out how to teach and assess "all" the information and skills of any science, history, health and/or music topic. Sometimes we default to what we are interested in or skilled at as teachers, resort to previous practice, or make decisions to cover what is supported by available resources.

So where does that leave us? Based on our work with teams of teachers across subject and grade levels, we would like to share two starting points:

1. Map the inquiry skills and dispositions onto the assessment and evaluation tools that are mandated in your school board, district, province, or state. Reproducible 2D, *An inquiry rubric* provides a sample framework of how inquiry can be assessed and evaluated according to the domains of knowledge, thinking, communication and application. In your jurisdiction there may be other domains and expectations mandated by the curriculum.

2. Identify the inquiry learning in your curriculum and begin your initial planning there. Some curricula (e.g., math, science, social studies and language arts) are very explicit at identifying the inquiry skills and processes to be developed. In others, inquiry is not named explicitly, but can be found in critical thinking expectations, research and problem-solving processes, collaborative work skills, innovation, and other creative processes. If you are new to inquiry learning, you may want to start small, perhaps with a particular topic. If you are more experienced, think of ways to extend inquiry learning and increase student choice and independence in an entire subject or series of inquiries.

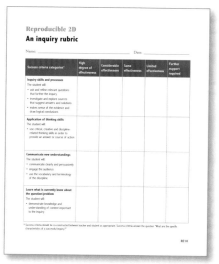

FIGURE 2.5 Reproducible 2D, p. RE10.

Mapping out explicit and implicit inquiry skills across subject areas is a valuable conversation between colleagues who teach in the junior division. Consider using the six essential inquiry abilities as a framework in which to group and consolidate your required curriculum standards. If, for example, you and your colleagues decide to target "questioning" as the first essential inquiry ability you want to foster in your students, then you may want to develop criteria related to questioning and design an assessment tool to target those criteria. See Reproducible 3E, *Assessment planning template: Asks questions* on p. RE19 as an example.

Literacy and numeracy skills are easily incorporated into inquiry learning. Many teachers find that a single topic or unit in science, social studies, history, geography, dramatic arts, health and well-being are a good place to introduce or expand inquiry thinking for their students. Some teachers plan to set aside a certain amount of time per week to encourage students to pursue their own inquiries independently (this independent inquiry time has diverse names such as "personal passion projects" or a "genius hour").

In sum, curriculum should be regarded as a means, not an end. If our aim is for students to engage in rich, personally and socially significant learning activities that target big ideas and enduring understandings, then the items that make up curriculum become the means by which to carry out this learning. Simply put, knowledge of the legal system is important if you are committed to addressing an injustice in your community.

Inquiry learning reminds us of a basic fact; that what is known about any topic can only ever be regarded as provisional. Knowledge is always changing and in flux, as opposed to unquestionable; this is because the inquiry learners of the world create and build upon this knowledge.

THINQ

- How could you and your colleagues begin to plan meaningful inquiry assessment based on the six essential abilities?
- Connect with other educators who use "genius hours," "personal passion projects" or other types of integrated inquiry learning. Share your thinking and promote inquiry learning to a wider professional audience.
- Where are the explicit and implicit inquiry skills and dispositions in your curriculum and in recent evidence-based education trends?

THINQ BIG

Leveraging knowledge and expertise in your school and beyond

There are some jurisdictions in the world whose curricula and assessments are profoundly different and more "inquiry-friendly" than our own (and there are also many that are less "inquiry-friendly").

You may know of classrooms, schools or districts that are more inquiry-focused in their learning environments and curriculum documents. These places of inquiry are important sources of inspiration and information. Remind yourself that education systems are changing when you feel frustrated and constricted by external mandates that do not encourage inquiry learning.

CONVICTION
Do you and your colleagues see your inquiry efforts as a contribution to a long-term change in the education system?

2.3 How can we partner with our students in assessment?

Assessment and learning activities should be as seamless as possible; otherwise, students will come to see assessment as something that is "done to them" in a potentially negative way, instead of as a helpful and natural part of improving as a learner.

Assessment partnerships

Students should be our assessment partners. They should have a say in what to aim for, what quality looks like, and provide choices in how to demonstrate their learning. Authentic snapshots of learning are made possible these days by new technologies that allow students to capture their thinking to share with peers, teachers and parents. These technologies open up new possibilities of assessment documentation.

We would suggest using the six essential inquiry abilities as a place to begin your assessment partnership with your students. Together, you can progressively detail what quality "looks like" in each of the six abilities. You can "check-in" with students on their growth in the six inquiry abilities. Students can be part of the discussion on what type of evidence they might want to show to demonstrate that they are meeting the criteria of quality in each ability. The use of an inquiry journal (digital, audio and/or written) that provides evidence of the six abilities may help you and your students in your inquiry assessment partnership.

Our ultimate goal in inquiry assessment is for students to internalize criteria for quality in all six essential inquiry abilities so that they can judge their own inquiry work. For example, in early junior grades, a student may not understand how the criteria of logic can apply to asking questions. As they have opportunities to ask questions and to work with the concept of logic, they hopefully would rethink posing the question "Does shouting lead to thinness?" since they would realize that the question is not logical. The question might be fun, playful and imaginative, but it is not logical.

BIG IDEA
Students should be our assessment partners.

TECH-ENABLED INQUIRY

Mobile technologies and balanced assessment

Today, ubiquitous student and teacher access to smartphones and tablets offers unprecedented opportunities for students to become real assessment partners. Observation of and conversations about in-the-moment learning can be easily captured by and shared with students using handheld devices. Teachers need not be the only ones with the responsibility and capacity to collect and consider evidence of learning — now students can too.

Gathering and assessing video evidence facilitates direct student involvement in their learning. Students can assess their own or a peer's performance during formative assessments, and make the necessary adjustments to improve their work. Teachers need to consider how all students can become reliable, autonomous self-assessors, as well as independent adjustors of their own performance.

In the same way, if students were asked to create questions about recycling and its impact on the environment (and not on human psychology), they would dismiss the potential question "Does recycling make people happy or sad?" since it is an irrelevant question to the topic under consideration. This junior learner has successfully internalized some of the important criteria for quality in asking questions. They know that questions should be logical and relevant and can apply this knowledge to their learning independently. This student may then work on a deeper understanding of other quality criteria for questions (e.g., questions that provoke interest, demand deep thinking, consider other viewpoints, etc.). Reproducible 2E, *Essential inquiry vocabulary* offers a list of vocabulary words, such as "relevant" and "logical," to encourage a shared understanding of inquiry learning.

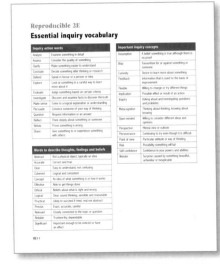

FIGURE 2.6 Reproducible 2E, p. RE11.

Allow students to co-construct criteria for quality, when appropriate, in order to demystify assessment and to guarantee that students know exactly what is expected of them. Sometimes it is most appropriate for the teacher who has the most experience and expertise in judging quality to suggest criteria of quality and then to allow students to work with these criteria until they understand and internalize them. Avoid complicated jargon, wordy criteria, and use only words and phrases that students can understand.

Criteria for quality are a work in progress in the classroom. This is a good thing, as it acknowledges that as our understanding deepens through each inquiry experience, we can decide together to change, drop or add criteria. Sometimes we can see quality in a new way, in the creative and powerful works of our students. Note in Figure 2.7 how criteria for quality in inquiry might develop over time as students and teachers deepen and clarify their understanding of what quality looks like.

> **CONVICTION**
> How do you feel about students being "partners in assessment"?

What is a quality argument?	
Initial thinking	**Revised thinking**
• It makes sense.	• The conclusion is clear and makes sense (logical).
• The information about the topic is persuasive.	• The arguments are plausible (reasonable and not impossible).
• There is a lot of supporting detail.	• The supporting evidence is accurate and relevant.
	• It is persuasive because it considers the strengths and weaknesses of other points of view.

FIGURE 2.7 The criteria for evaluating a quality argument might change over time.

Here are a few points of caution regarding creating criteria for quality in an inquiry. Whether on your own or when co-constructing with your students, do not confuse criteria for quality with other product "requirements." For example, you may decide to assess an inquiry learner's ability to give and ask for reasons through the creation of a multimedia product. The main criteria of quality of this multimedia product must focus on the understanding of, communication of, and application of reasoning; not on the length, use of colour, or other specifications of the multimedia product that are not fundamental to reasoning. The focus should be on building assessment tools that are linked to learning rather than task completion.

Similarly, be clear with students that quantity doesn't equal quality. This is true of questions, reasons, supporting evidence and contributions to collaborative conversations. Students may hold the misconception that "doing more" equates with quality.

And lastly, avoid too many criteria for quality, since a long list may confuse and discourage learners and often reflects our own confusion about what is important in inquiry learning.

A feedback-rich classroom

Research on the importance of formative assessment details how effective feedback can increase student learning. Providing effective feedback is the one crucial strategy of formative assessment. When feedback is accepted and acted on by the learner, it leads to higher achievement.

Feedback is not merely advice or praise, nor is it merely highlighting mistakes or deficiencies. Feedback should be specific to inquiry learning skills and dispositions, and helpful to each individual learner in that it provides a suggested action to take.

Giving feedback is a sophisticated skill since all learners are vulnerable when receiving it. Only in a classroom with trust and respect, in addition to specific and intentional norms of collaboration, can a learner welcome feedback. Feedback should make the learner think and must be offered in a supportive and timely fashion.

CONTEXT
How would your students say you define quality learning?

CONVICTION
Are you convinced by the research that indicates feedback is a critical strategy for improving student learning?

One way to cultivate a feedback-rich classroom is by establishing a common understanding of inquiry dispositions and of the criteria for quality in inquiry thinking and skills. This common understanding allows students to be partners in assessment conversations. They can then offer effective feedback to themselves and to others, after it has been directly taught and modelled by the teacher.

This direct instruction and modelling of effective feedback is sometimes overlooked. Students may default to giving vague and unhelpful praise ("I like your poster.") or criticism ("Your point doesn't make sense."). These statements cannot be acted upon because the assessor either does not understand the purpose or qualities of effective feedback, or cannot apply them since they have not had adequate instruction or practice to do so.

Students should also be taught how to question feedback ("What do you mean when you say you like it?") and politely question (and possibly reject) unreasonable feedback ("I gave three strong arguments; why don't you think they are strong?") since this ability dovetails with inquiry reasoning skills.

A feedback rich classroom is built on reciprocity. As a student, if I am given the chance to provide other learners with feedback, this opportunity allows me to both share in their learning and to reflect on my own. Getting feedback from others allows for "fresh eyes" on my work and enables a caring conversation that will affect our mutual understanding of criteria for quality. I expect that my fellow learners will give their best efforts at feedback and I will respond accordingly by improving my work since I value and appreciate their efforts on behalf of my learning.

A helpful rule of thumb is that the learner receiving the feedback should be expected to work harder than the learner (or teacher) who is giving it. Figure 2.8 provides a list of suggestions on how to use feedback effectively during inquiry learning.

CONFIRMATION

Do your preferences for receiving professional feedback align with what we advocate for students?

CONTEXT

Do you sometimes feel that you spend more time giving feedback than students do addressing it?

INQUIRY IN ACTION

Is it good feedback?

A student in your class has just participated in a collaborative group discussion. Consider these possible statements you could offer the students, and think about which one actually offers helpful feedback.

1. Why didn't you participate more? You're very quiet.

2. I know you can do better next time. You're usually the best in the group.

3. Tell me in what ways did you contribute effectively to the group discussion?

4. I heard you building on other people's ideas but I didn't hear you defending your idea. Next time, be sure to defend your own idea with reasons and evidence.

5. What might you have said today in this group that you did not?

If you selected the fourth statement, you are correct. This statement is relatively easy to identify due to its specificity. It also gives the student the opportunity to talk about their thinking with their teacher so that the teacher can provide additional feedback and encouragement as required.

1. Use technology (e.g., audio, video, photos and document sharing) to facilitate "real time" self and peer feedback.

2. When posting the criteria of quality work for a particular inquiry, be sure to return to the list throughout an inquiry process to allow students to revise the list based on new learning in the class.

3. Provide students with exemplars of work and ask them to provide written or oral feedback based on one or two criteria. Take samples of the feedback and use it for a class discussion on the qualities of effective feedback.

4. Highlight (do not annotate) a student's written work and return it to them, asking them to determine what criteria of quality was highlighted and how it could be improved.

5. Ask students to highlight in their written work their arguments and supporting evidence in different colours as a way to see at a glance if they are meeting important overall criteria.

6. When students submit work to you, ask them to identify one criteria that they would like for you to provide feedback on (this feedback could differ from criteria used in self or peer assessment).

7. Provide students with checklists of basic requirements that they must complete before work is assessed. Return work that does not meet the checklist requirements (do not assess it). Checklist requirements may include: the work is word-processed; the work has been proofread; the work includes a title, a main argument and three sources (at least one from a library book), etc.

8. Postpone, for as long as possible, putting levels, marks or grades on assessment pieces. Descriptive feedback is what is most helpful for the learner at this stage.

9. If a student is not responding to feedback, ask them if they need something to be re-taught or re-explained and/or provide other emotional-social supports.

10. Encourage students to explain criteria and ask for feedback from parents, guardians and caregivers.

11. Ask yourself *before* you provide extensive written feedback to students whether the learner has had opportunities to self-assess based on criteria for quality that they understand?

FIGURE 2.8 There are many ways to provide effective feedback to your students.

Determining what my students already know about inquiry

An important part of assessment is determining the prior inquiry experience your students have had and the specific inquiry learning skills they have developed. It is easy to dive straight into inquiry activities without first considering if students understand the difference between a summary and a synthesis, a question and a hypothesis, or a deep question versus a shallow one.

Reproducible 2F, *Student exploration: Can you identity an argument?* and Reproducible 2G, *Student exploration: Errors in thinking and logic* are activities that may help you gather information on students' knowledge and understanding of inquiry qualities before they are asked to apply understanding in more sophisticated ways. Reproducible 2D, *An inquiry rubric* may help you determine if your students can identify an argument versus an explanation, opinion or observation. Your students may come to school with the preconception that arguments are verbal conflicts between two people (and that the person who yells the loudest wins).

This common preconception is a natural starting place for you to unpack and develop the concept of argument as an essential part of reasoning and as a skill that allows learners to make sense of the world by creating arguments and considering the arguments of others.

Your observation of students as they complete the activities in Reproducibles 2F and 2G and the resulting conversations you have may assist you in determining whether direct instruction, further examples or practice are required, or whether students can move on to develop their own arguments and are capable of recognizing arguments from more complicated sources such as the Internet. You may even consider having students summarize their understanding of an argument (and/ or the qualities of a good argument) in their own words and/or through a key visual in an inquiry journal. Taking a photo of their visual or text summary could be a powerful piece of assessment data for you.

Reproducible 2G, *Student exploration: Errors in thinking and logic* is a suggested starting place to observe students' understanding of what they think is strong or weak thinking. You may be surprised at the significant skill students have in recognizing strong thinking. They may not be familiar with the dozens of Latin terms for fallacies of thought, but they can explain the problem or weakness in the thinking. The challenge for students and adults alike is to become more self-reflective and recognize when we are not thinking "well." It's always easier to detect weaknesses in someone else's thinking.

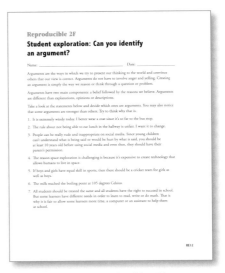

FIGURE 2.9 Reproducible 2F, p. RE12.

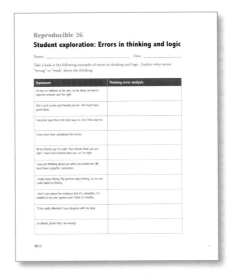

FIGURE 2.10 Reproducible 2G, p. RE13.

THINQ

• What methods of feedback do you feel most confident with? Which new methods of feedback would you like to try and why?

• How do you create classroom conditions where students are effective, comfortable and confident in giving, accepting and questioning feedback?

• Do you provide your students with opportunities to explain what an inquiry is and how to determine an effective inquiry?

• How do your students understand "strong" and "weak" thinking? How could you deepen their understanding through an inquiry?

2.4 How do I gather, interpret and respond to assessment evidence?

Inquiry assessment is an iterative three-stage process: gathering, interpreting and responding to evidence of the quality of a student's inquiry skills and dispositions. We can feel confident in our inquiry assessment when we gather evidence of each student achieving their best work, interpret their understanding and skill fairly and accurately, and respond appropriately to their needs. This is a complex task.

Each learner is unique, so how do we plan to gather assessment evidence of inquiry learning in a way that is fair and supportive of every student's learning? One of the basic ways to make assessment fair and reflective for all students is to triangulate your assessment data. This means balancing your use of evidence taken from observations of the student, conversations with the student, and products of learning created by the student.

Balanced assessment

As teachers we have little problem coming up with an extensive list of potential products that could be used as assessment evidence.

Oral presentations, blogs, web pages, written reports, dioramas, constructing models, performances and artwork are just a few product examples. Yet these products are only valid as assessment evidence when the product genuinely reflects the student's best thinking and full understanding.

Many teachers can recall a student who was not particularly adept or motivated by completing a certain product. But in conversation with them or by observing them working on their own or collaboratively, we realized that they knew a lot more and had more skill than their product revealed. Teachers can react quickly to conversations and observations to provide timely and practical feedback.

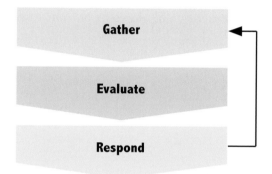

FIGURE 2.11 There are three stages to the inquiry assessment process.

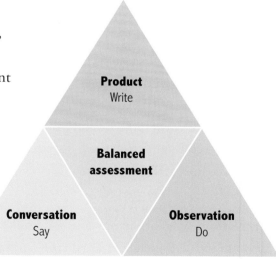

FIGURE 2.12 Balanced assessment means gathering evidence of learning through observation and conversation, not just completed products.

Observations and conversations are not only powerful as formative assessment but also as valid evidence for evaluation purposes. If a student demonstrates their ability to reason logically during small group discussions, then this evidence is valid. If they fail to reason logically with a similar problem in written form, they may require support with word choice, decoding text and/or confidence in their ability to write.

For some time in education, written products have been considered the most valuable source of assessment data. However current research points to student voice as one of the richest ways to accurately determine what a student knows. Student voice helps to inform the teacher and the student when, where and why thinking gets stuck and how best to move along.

The second stage of this iterative assessment process is to interpret evidence of learning. Some ways to increase the reliability of our subjective interpretations is to make sure the criteria of quality is understood by the learner in advance of the task and that feedback was provided based on that same criteria of quality.

We also need to reflect on our own biases and assumptions about our learners. It can be an eye-opening professional learning experience to assess student work without names on products or to work with colleagues to co-assess student thinking in the classroom. These opportunities can hone our skills at fair interpretation of student work.

At the third stage of the process, we should respond to the evidence of learning. Can we carry on with the next task confident in student's abilities, do we need provide additional feedback, or do we need to redesign our next teaching steps

INQUIRY IN ACTION

Same learning activity, different assessment choices

At the end of class, Joan gathers the written questions that students have created during collaborative discussions. One of the criteria for question quality is relevance. From the questions, she interprets that most students are having difficulty creating relevant questions based on the topic and concept under discussion. Many of the questions are irrelevant. Her response is to re-teach the term "relevant" the next day by modeling how to create relevant questions. She'll then give the students a selection of questions and ask them to identify ones that are relevant.

Marion's students also create questions collaboratively with relevance as an important criteria for quality. She observes her students creating the questions and has conversations with each group as they are working. She notices that only some of the students are struggling with creating relevant questions. She decides to have an informal "inquiry huddle" with those students where she addresses their misunderstandings. She also asks students who are proficient in the skill to act as learning resources for those who are just emerging in their abilities.

These two teachers had the same intention, to teach the importance of relevance in asking questions, but their documentation and next steps differed. This illustrates the fact that there are many options in terms of gathering and acting on assessment evidence. Triangulation helps to ensure that you have a more complete picture of a student's best work.

THINQ

- How did Joan and Marion differ in their assessments?
- What are the advantages, possibilities and challenges to their methods of assessment gathering and their responses to assessment evidence?
- What questions remain?

entirely? At each of the three stages, our decisions may positively or negatively impact our goal of gathering evidence of each student achieving their best work at a given point in time.

This is the creative art of teaching — deciding what instructional and formative assessment method is best for your learners. One of the great qualities of inquiry learning is that it provides ample time to observe and have conversations with students while they are proceeding through an inquiry.

Communicating with parents

Building parental support for an inquiry-based classroom and school is critical. Classroom newsletters should celebrate and clarify what deep learning looks like in your classroom. School newsletters offer a school wide-vision of inquiry learning and may help to alleviate fears or misconceptions parents may have regarding inquiry learning. Parents need to see the benefits of this approach and be invited to participate in its implementation. Using classroom blogs and other social media to share student artifacts resulting from inquiry learning help parents to appreciate and support what may be viewed as a new type of learning. In terms of assessment, using clear and "jargon-less" communication to inform parents of their child's learning is appreciated.

Evaluation

Summative assessment, evaluation or assessment of learning is a learner's opportunity to show their best work at an "end point." What the end point is and when it is reached involves judgment based on standards. Generally, after multiple opportunities to explore and make sense of an inquiry question, problem, skill or disposition, it is time for an evaluation.

Evaluations should not involve new skills, new understandings, new tasks or new criteria of quality. Evaluation is a repeat performance of learning activities that were previously assessed. They should not include additional layers of complexity that are new to the learner.

Sample parental communication

In this sample communication, note how Barry's strengths as an inquiry learner are the focus. These strengths are interwoven with observations of his understanding and application of content knowledge, his use of skills (inquiry skills and other skills) and his ability to set personal goals for his own learning.

"Barry wants to know more about space exploration and our solar system. He asks important, relevant and deep questions. He is motivated to answer his questions. He understands the scientific facts and theories about the solar system and how this interacts with space travel. He sets goals for his learning after reflecting on his challenges (procrastination and organization of notes) and successes (persevering and understanding what is known about the topic). He applied his learning to a creative presentation entitled "Should we continue space travel?" He worked collaboratively with his group to communicate ideas and conclusions. He encouraged others to become curious and interested in space exploration."

FIGURE 2.13 This a sample of what communicating the results of an inquiry learning unit to parents could look like.

Our advice is to hold off on evaluation as long as possible. We realize that report cards and external pressures for marks can make this advice challenging. However, a teacher who regularly documents assessment evidence will have more than enough information on how the student is learning before specifically quantifying that learning against a mandated standard. In the following chapters on *Wondering and questioning*, *Investigating and exploring*, and *Making sense*, specific practical ideas will be offered regarding assessment and evaluation in each of these inquiry phases.

Planning

We encourage you to work with colleagues to create, implement and revise an inquiry assessment plan through frequent opportunities for professional reflection. An inquiry assessment plan, in brief, is an outline of your intentions based on key questions. Prior agreement with your colleagues as to the answers to these questions is important, but the route that is taken to achieve these shared goals is always dependent upon the emergent properties of learning in your classroom with your individual students. This is because the outcome of any inquiry activity cannot be completely known or detailed in advance.

We suggest using these questions as a starting point of conversation with your colleagues in planning a unit of inquiry. The inquiry assessment plan should be returned to and additional detail added as the unit unfolds. Keep it simple. Too many goals, skills or criteria along with too much content will confuse your students and make your interpretation of evidence daunting and

TEACHER QUERIES

Shouldn't students know the content and have the skills before beginning an inquiry?

At times we are asked to weigh in with an opinion on whether the "how," or the process with which a student applies inquiry skills and dispositions, is more important that the "what," or the specific content knowledge that is required in the inquiry.

This age-old content versus skills debate is unhelpful. Inquiry learning is a critical assessment and application of what is already known about a topic, synthesized in new ways to build new knowledge to answer a question or problem. Teachers who claim they must wait until students "know the content" before conducting an inquiry are confused about what inquiry learning is. Teachers who claim that content knowledge is not important to an inquiry are also confused about what inquiry learning is.

Another sticking point for teachers in inquiry learning is the desire to have students master inquiry skills before entering into an inquiry learning unit. This is an impossible aim because the development of inquiry skills comes from doing inquiry and is ongoing. Moreover, all learners continue to further develop their inquiry skills despite their years of experience and expertise. As outlined in Chapter 1, inquiry learning is constructivist; the learner is "doing" science, "doing" math and "doing" history in a developmentally appropriate way. The learner is not a passive witness watching the teacher "talking about" the subject or topic or memorizing information.

The final sticky point of inquiry assessment involves the timing of assessment. Assessment practices of the past were typically "add-ons" at certain points, usually the "end" of a unit of study. Now we view assessment not as events, but as everyday classroom experiences where we show what we know, what we can do, look for advice and feedback, and provide the same for ourselves and our peers.

- How will I get to know my students so that inquiry activities will be purposeful and meaningful to them?

- How can I stretch and extend my students' curiosity and interests in terms of curricular topics and subjects?

- What is the real question or fundamental problem of the inquiry?

- What is the goal of this inquiry (e.g., consider key concepts, inquiry skills, inquiry dispositions, supporting content and corresponding curriculum expectations)?

- How will I sustain student curiosity and interest, voice and choice, diversity and originality?

- What opportunities will I provide for practice and feedback?

- What do I predict may be the areas of greatest student support?

- What are key misconceptions and preconceptions about this concept, topic, phenomenon or process?

- What are the criteria of quality for this inquiry?

- How will I support each student's learning during this inquiry?

- What quality evidence will I gather of student learning for this inquiry?

- How (and when) will I judge student achievement of this inquiry?

FIGURE 2.14 You can use these questions as a starting point for planning an inquiry unit.

unmanageable. Even the most sophisticated inquiry learners do not require a plan filled with "more." For those learners, the standard of quality that you will expect may differ.

THINQ

- What would a reasonable, manageable and valid evaluation of an inquiry entail?

- In what ways could you make the demonstration of quality inquiry skills the most important part of a culminating evaluation?

- How might you manage the dual goals of consistent assessment amongst classes of the same grade with the importance of fairness in terms of specific classroom contexts and individual student needs?

- How might your school explain to family members why inquiry-based learning is important in today's world and how it can be meaningfully assessed and evaluated?

> **COMMITMENT**
> Do "sticky" assessment problems limit your commitment to or implementation of inquiry-based learning?

Revisit and reflect

Assessment and inquiry learning were braided together in this chapter. Six essential inquiry abilities were offered as a way to anchor your assessment planning and communication with students. Three assumptions of the chapter were that:

- assessment improves both teaching and learning,

- assessment must be multi-faceted in nature, and

- inquiry is a dynamic process where learners assess themselves and each other on a regular basis.

The fact that all learners can recognize and respond to the learning while it is taking place during an inquiry is what inquiry assessment is all about.

THINQ

- What type of assessment evidence do you gather from your students? Do you feel you have balanced evidence from triangulated sources? How might you address an imbalance, if there is one?

- How might you strengthen student self-assessment of inquiry dispositions?

- In what ways could you make your students partners in inquiry assessment?

- What are the possibilities of inquiry assessment in your classroom? What are the challenges? How might you address head-on or work around the challenges?

- Complete Reproducible 2H, *Teacher checklist: Purposeful planning for inquiry* to further your thinking on effective assessment planning.

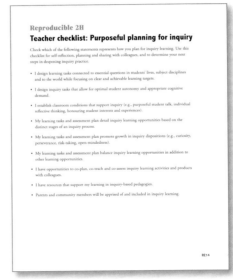

BIG IDEAS

2.1 At the heart of assessment are teachers and students asking, "How are we doing?"

2.2 Curriculum should be seen not as the end, but as the means to engage students in rich learning activities.

2.3 Students should be our assessment partners.

2.4 Inquiry assessment involves gathering, interpreting and responding to evidence of a student's inquiry skills and dispositions.

FIGURE 2.15 Reproducible 2H, p. RE14.

Chapter 3

WONDERING AND QUESTIONING:

The key to inquiry learning

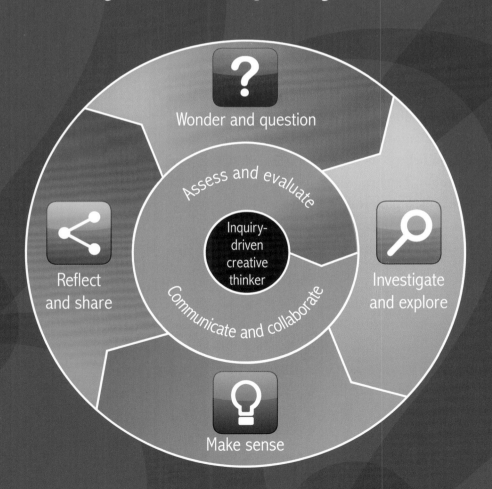

3.1 How can I nurture wonder in my classroom?

Inquiry begins with wondering. Learning begins with questions. We are all curious about the way the world works. Our curiosity fuels our learning. Our curiosity provides purpose to our learning.

We can sense when wonder is at work in our students. They are both fascinated and focused. Questions arise. Imagination and critical thought transpire. At these moments, the learner feels excited and determined to dive deeper into their learning.

How can we plan and prepare our classroom activities to allow students to become skilled questioners? How can we honour questions and position questions at the forefront of learning?

From wonder to questioning

A classroom filled with wonder seems ideal. A classroom filled with students asking lots of questions may make us feel a bit tentative. This tentativeness is understandable. Giving students the skills and opportunities to become questioners gives them more power and freedom as learners. This learner autonomy may be in tension with your beliefs (or widespread system beliefs) on the role of a student and the role of a teacher in the classroom. Teachers who strive to make their classrooms as democratic as possible are more comfortable with lots of questioning. Teachers who have lived through and adopted a more traditional and managerial approach to their classroom may feel at odds with promoting questioning as the anchor of learning.

Teachers have to feel confident in their co-learning stance with students in order to welcome questions to the fullest. Students need to know that in a caring and supportive inquiry community, questions should not be used to distract, belittle, bully or embarrass others. Instead, questions should be used to reflect our curiosities and drive learning. Similarly, teachers shouldn't ignore, deflect or discourage students' questions but encourage, stimulate and respect them. Student questions reveal three very important things to teachers: what students know, what students don't know and who they are. Questions reveal interests, fears, hopes, concerns, likes and dislikes.

BIG IDEA

Our curiosity fuels our learning.

CONVICTION

What are your beliefs about the relationship between wondering, questioning and learning in your classroom?

FOOD FOR THOUGHT

"Learn from yesterday, live for today, hope for tomorrow. The important thing is to not stop questioning."
Albert Einstein

"Thinking is not driven by answers. It is driven by questions."
Richard Paul and Linda Elder

"The power to question is the basis of all human progress."
Indira Gandhi

"In mathematics the art of proposing a question must be held of higher value than solving it."
Georg Cantor

Questioning plays centre stage in an inquiry. It is the one of the six essential abilities of inquiry learners. Questioning also intersects and supports the other five essential abilities. You cannot show curiosity without questions. Questions for different purposes and different perspectives demonstrate open mindedness. Asking for reasons compliments the skill of giving reasons. Understanding what is currently known and putting it all together involves questioning authority, being skeptical and assessing sources. And lastly, there is no thinking together without questioning together.

Questioning that develops learning

Without questions, there is no inquiry learning. Questions guide us through our thinking. In education, answers are privileged over questions. Textbooks, resources, web pages and teachers are filled with answers. But we want students to see the questions behind the information, arguments and theories. Only then can students see that knowledge is created actively, not received passively.

Students need to recognize that some questions can lead to a dead end. Sometimes a question must be abandoned or reformulated into a completely new one. Questions also lead to more questions. There is no end to the questioning process.

Here are a few examples to get you started:

- **Post your essential course inquiry questions** in a conspicuous place. Allow for students to build on and add to these questions. Build assessments and evaluation around the process of answering the question.

- **Utilize social media** and blogs as a way for students to ask and answer questions.

- **Model your own curiosities** and questions. Pose powerful questions of your own and encourage students to do the same.

- Provide students with Reproducible 4C, *Evaluating sources and evidence: U.S.E. I.T.* where they can **record questions** that arise after viewing a source or hearing a community speaker.

CAPACITY
How would you assess your willingness and capacity to take a co-learning stance with your students?

CONTEXT
What role do questions currently play in the context of your daily instructional practice? What questions are asked? Who asks them and for what purpose?

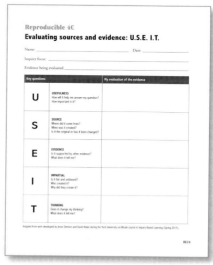

FIGURE 3.1 Reproducible 4C, p. RE24.

- **Feature a "question of the day"** and briefly consider how and where you could start answering the question.

- **Convert into questions**, portions of a text, a diagram of a structure or a math solution.

- **Create a question wall** where students post their questions. Change the layout of the question wall as student understanding changes. For example:

  - Create a **continuum of questions** (from left-to-right or top-to-bottom) starting with factual or "closed" questions moving to deeper, "open-ended" questions.

  - Pose and **post group questions** on the wall according to the purpose of the question (e.g., factual, evaluative, comparative, causal, predictive, inquiry), the "lens" of the question (e.g., ethical, economic legal, scientific, environmental, mathematical, cultural, social, political, etc.) or through different personal, social, cultural, national, community or natural perspectives.

  - Have students come up with their **own criteria** for the sorting and layout of the questions.

- **Create a question kite** with the main inquiry question at the top and resulting questions on the kite's "tail."

- Use **community circles** where you and students ask questions together.

- Keep a **curiosity corner** where students can begin to answer chosen questions from the question wall.

- Use **KWHLAQ charts** (Reproducible 3A, *KWHLAQ charts*) at appropriate stages of the inquiry.

- Use Reproducible 3B, *Student exploration: Why question?* to have students identify and extend their understanding of the **purposes of questioning**.

CONTEXT
Have you used any of these activities to honour questions in your classroom? If so, what were the results?

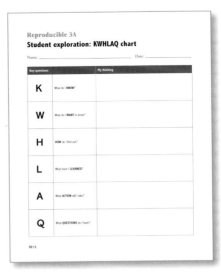

FIGURE 3.2 Reproducible 3A, p. RE15.

FIGURE 3.3 Reproducible 3B, p. RE16.

3.2 How can inquiry questions drive learning?

BIG IDEA

The purpose of an inquiry question is to entice your students to think deeply about the mysteries of life.

An inquiry question is a special type of question that helps drive units of learning. The purpose of an inquiry question is to entice your students to think deeply about the mysteries of life. These mysteries can be categorized by subject disciplines but are often interdisciplinary in nature (see Figure 3.4). As you read the sample inquiry questions, identify the core concepts and consider possible supporting content that you would use to plan an inquiry based on an inquiry question.

We hope that as you read through these sample questions, your curiosity and inquisitiveness was sparked. Inquiry questions are helpful to learners because they stimulate thinking and feeling, and they drive learning by signalling what is truly essential and fascinating. They can often be deceptively simple, but they cannot be simply answered.

CAPACITY

How confident are you in your understanding of the qualities of a good inquiry question? What else would you like to know?

FIGURE 3.4 There are no "right" inquiry questions, only inquiry questions that stimulate thought, discussion and drive learning.

Questions that drive learning	
Interdisciplinary questions • Who am I? • Are human beings naturally good? • Is there a best way to learn? • Is prejudice caused by ignorance or experience? • Who should lead? Who should follow?	**Social studies** • What makes a good community? • What makes a good friend? • Whom should we care for? • Do we need rules?
Literature/Media studies • How is language power? • How do you decide whether a book/website/movie/TV show is good? • Why should we read different authors from different places? • Should we care about literature, poetry, etc.? • How does the media shape our view of ourselves and the world?	**History** • Is history truth or fiction? • How can we better understand the people of the past? • How do we know what we know about the past? • What makes Canada's historical identity? • Why do we tell some people's stories but not other's? • When should we fight? • What is fair in economics, politics, law, sports, etc.?

The arts
- What is beautiful?
- Why do people dance/make art/make music?
- Is there a "right way" to make art?
- How can motion express emotion?
- Should artists care about what their audiences think?
- Is there a best way to give feedback to an artist?

Geography
- What is where, why there, and why care? (Coined by Charles Gritzner)
- Why does Canada look the way it does?
- Why do people disagree about how to use resources?
- Is it possible to create sustainable communities?
- What is the geography of your life?

Math
- What strategies can be used to continue a sequence, solve for an unknown, etc.?
- How can information be gathered, recorded and organized?
- How can we test predictions?
- How can you make a reasonable estimate?
- Where are patterns in nature, architecture, music, words and numbers?
- Why are graphs (e.g., probability, grouping, etc.) helpful?
- What types of problems are solved with measurement?
- How can fractions help me in real life?

Science
- Will science save us from using up our natural resources?
- What is my responsibility to the environment?
- How do we know if scientific theories are correct?
- How does science use evidence?
- Why should we recognize patterns that exist in our world?
- How do we distinguish "good" science from "bad" science?
- How are structure and function related in living things?
- Is aging a bad thing?

World religions
- What makes God, God?
- What is compassion, truth, free will, sin, etc.?
- How do the sacred writings of the world religions inform my life?
- How certain should we be about our beliefs?
- What virtues make a moral life possible?
- How does one become a better Jew, Christian, Muslim, Buddhist, Hindu, humanist, etc.?
- What is faith and its role in the human search for meaning and truth?
- Can we prove that God exists?

Health and well being
- Will my generation live until we're 150 years old?
- How does our society define health?
- How do I define a healthy life?
- Is stress always bad?
- How does eating affect me?
- How safe are my food choices?
- Why are some people afraid to talk about mental illness?

In their book *Essential Questions*, Jay McTighe and Grant Wiggins (2013) make the case for teachers to collaboratively create inquiry (or essential) questions. The use of questions signals to students that inquiry is the goal of learning in your class, and makes it more likely that a unit of study will be intellectually engaging. The use of questions also forces us to clarify and prioritize what is truly important in terms of learning for our students.

Qualities of an effective inquiry question

The qualities of an effective inquiry question are detailed in John Barell's book *Developing More Curious Minds* (2003). A good inquiry question: is an invitation to think (not recall, summarize or detail); comes from genuine curiosity and confusion about the world; makes you think about something in a way you may have never considered before; invites both deep thinking and deep feelings; leads to more good questions; and asks you to think critically, creatively, ethically, purposefully and reflectively about essential ideas in a discipline.

There are many places to find great inquiry questions: in curriculum documents, teacher and student resources, and in online teacher resources. Great inquiry questions are difficult to create from scratch, so we would suggest looking to your board, school and online resources to generate inquiry questions that would be appropriate to anchor and drive learning for the school year, an entire subject area, or a particular unit of study. We suggest that groups of educators take time to find, develop, revise and choose inquiry questions that are appropriate for their classrooms. This is the starting place for an inquiry-friendly learning community.

An effective inquiry question...

1 ... is an invitation to think (not recall, summarize or detail).	2 ... comes from genuine curiosity and/or confusion about the world.
3 ... makes you think about something in a way you haven't before.	4 ... invites both deep thinking and deep feelings.
5 ... leads to more good questions.	6 ... asks you to think about the essential ideas in a discipline.

FIGURE 3.5 The most effective inquiry questions share common qualities that make them exciting, provocative, and intellectually challenging.

Have students develop their own inquiry questions

Getting students to ask intellectually engaging and fascinating inquiry questions is vital to their development as autonomous learners beyond the classroom. Reproducible 3C, *Student exploration: Asking questions arising from provocations* can help students create effective inquiry questions by understanding the criteria for what makes an effective inquiry question. You may wish to introduce criteria one or two items at a time and make an anchor chart of student answers for reference, providing time to use it with feedback prior to adding additional criteria.

However, before attempting to create their own inquiry questions, we would suggest getting students confident and comfortable with asking as many questions as they can by beginning with wonder activities and provocations. In section 3.3, we outline the characteristics of wonder activities and provide examples.

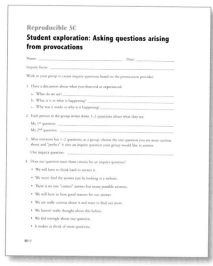

FIGURE 3.6 Reproducible 3C, p. RE17.

3.3 What does inquiry questioning look like?

Teachers have creative and novel ideas on how to stimulate student interest. We are always striving to ignite learning by getting students to think about something in a new way. We'll refer to these creative and novel ideas developed by teachers as "wonder activities" or provocations, as coined by Reggio Emilia practitioners.

Wonder activities: Questioning to ignite learning

Even though your students will not all respond with the same intensity to each wonder activity or provocation, three important learnings are intended. First, when participating in the activity, they get to witness how other learners respond with different levels of emotion, curiosity and open-mindedness. Secondly, they note how other learners have distinct knowledge to share and that collaboration is an effective way to learn. Lastly, and perhaps most importantly, regular wonder activities or provocations point to how the world is a place filled with curiosities just waiting for their active engagement.

Some of the wonder activities teachers use may cause amazement, like a scientific experiment, while others may trigger outrage, like real-life stories of injustice. These places of strong emotion are undoubtedly the best place to begin.

Students should understand that wonder activities are a springboard for their questions and an opportunity to build on the questions posed by others. It is also an opportunity to share what you know and to listen to what others know. In addition, reasoning — in response to the phenomenon under consideration — is a crucial aim.

Wonder activities can be used to deepen specific inquiry skills and dispositions. They can also be used to power learning on a particular curriculum topic or concept.

Wonder activities or provocations can be brief, engaging the emotions and curiosity of a learner while also introducing something new or causing them to look at something in a new way. Wonder activities are distinguished from traditional "lesson hooks" or "minds on"

BIG IDEA
Questions that elicit strong emotions are often the best place to begin.

CONTEXT
What are your students typically most curious about? What types of questions might stimulate them?

TEACHER QUERIES

What about students who do not like to question?

Getting to know our students is important for great inquiry learning. Students may feel that asking questions is rude, indiscreet or improper in some way. They may associate asking questions with "looking stupid." They also may not be used to asking questions in a classroom and feel that it is the role of the teacher to pose the questions. Have conversations with students, parents and caregivers regarding the role and purpose of asking questions in order for your learning community to flourish. Reproducible 3B, *Student exploration: Why question?* may assist in student-parent-teacher dialogue on the various important purposes of questions.

activities in that they should always involve time for students to have meaningful conversations in which they generate and build on each other's questions and give and ask for reasons for the phenomenon under consideration. Take your cue from students as to when to bring wonder activities to a close.

These activities can also be an anchor for a series of learning activities or they can sustain a unit of study where the questions created and reasons offered (or problems posed and solutions offered) are returned to and built upon as what is known is discovered, multiple perspectives are considered, and conclusions are shared. The following ideas are offered as suggestions in your planning of wonder activities.

You may want to use a framework such as the "I see, I think, I wonder, I feel" routine in Reproducible 3D, *Student exploration: What I see, what I think, what I wonder, what I feel* to cue students to the objectives of a wonder activity. Those objectives are to make careful observations, to articulate their feelings, to ask questions, and to propose reasoned preliminary explanations based on what they already know.

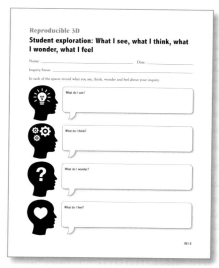

FIGURE 3.7 Reproducible 3D, p. RE18.

FIGURE 3.8 You may want to try different approaches to wonder to see which ones your students respond to. It may differ from person to person and class to class.

Wonder activities or provocations for the junior classroom

- **Pose an ethical dilemma** involving a topic of student interest (e.g., Should animals be used for research? Should children never be allowed to work for wages? Should there be a ban on energy drinks?).

- **Share a personal story**, statistic, infographic, law or historical fact that highlights social injustice (one that prompts student response such as "That's not fair!" or "That's so wrong!").

- **Play different types of music**, unfamiliar instruments and unique arrangements of known songs.

- **Share a family story** in which you share your curiosity by asking questions (e.g., I wonder how it felt to leave the country, I wonder why my grandmother never went to school, etc.). Ask students who are comfortable with this type of sharing to do the same.

- **Share artwork** of different types and genres (e.g., sculptures, realistic portraits, cubism, etc.).

- **Provide dramatic, spectacular photographs** of nature (search award winning photos from National Geographic for this purpose).

- **Take students outdoors** to observe a natural phenomenon (with magnifying glasses, with telescopes, with sketch pads) for the purpose of careful observation.

- **Share pictures or video of curious things** (e.g., acrobatics, unusual animal friendships, inventions of the past, spectacular and unusual structures, animals responding to music, babies swimming underwater, magic and illusions).

- **Conduct a science experiment** and allow time for speculation before, during and after (e.g., inflating balloons with vinegar and baking soda, dyeing flowers with coloured water).

- **Set out various artifacts** of wonder (perhaps based on a theme or topic) and allow students to circulate, ask questions and make connections.

It is an important step to allow students time for individual quiet thinking and reflection. After what you consider to be an appropriate amount of time for individual thinking, students could share their questions, ideas and knowledge and create a "we see, we think, we wonder, we feel" synthesis. This "thinking together" stage extends and improves learning for all and should reflect on this experience as part of their growth as inquiry learners.

Assessing during a wonder activity

Students should appreciate the purpose of the wonder activity: to learn more about the world, its people and each other. They should ask important and relevant questions and be able to offer reasons. They should show genuine interest in other students' perspectives and attitudes. Students should also realize that some questions may never be fully answered and demonstrate openness to continual learning.

You could gather assessment evidence during wonder activities by observing students' work through the "I see, I think, I wonder, I feel" framework or a similar framework. Through observation of this process you may be able to determine answers to the following questions:

- How are the learners responding to this provocation?

- What questions are being posed?

- What do the questions reveal about the learner (i.e., who they are and what they know)?

- How can I use this information to better students' learning?

- How could some of these questions be incorporated into future learning activities?

- What reasons are being offered?

- How can I support student reasoning in the next steps of the inquiry?

- What misconceptions and preconceptions do students have of this phenomenon?

- What would be the next best step for learning?

THINQ BIG

Leveraging expertise at your school

During professional learning time focused on inquiry learning, consider devoting some time to discuss each of these questions.

1. What fascinates you about learning and the subjects that you teach?

2. What inquiry questions could help us teach and students learn?

3. How can we keep these inquiry questions at the forefront of learning and assessment?

4. What wonder activities or provocations have we used that get students engaged and how could they be improved, extended and shared with other colleagues?

5. How could we involve parents and community members in inquiry learning?

Mars One mission: A sample wonder activity

Getting students to ask questions provides you the opportunity to get to know a lot about them as learners and as people. Their questions will reveal what they know and don't know about a topic. Their questions will also reveal their personal interests.

Consider this example of a wonder activity through the lens of three teachers. Each teacher is presenting students with a set of visual representations of the Mars One mission. Mars One is a non-profit organization based in the Netherlands that aims to create a viable human colony on Mars by the year 2027. People from all walks of life can put their name forward to the selection committee that will choose the astronauts on this one-way flight to Mars. Mars One's mission design, according to its website, is in the "early mission concept phase."

One activity, different purposes

The teachers have chosen visuals of Mars One to act as a provocation for similar reasons. They are certain that their students' curiosity will be piqued due to the novelty and intrigue around future space travel. They feel that their students' curiosity could lead to greater engagement in learning. However, the three teachers plan to use the Mars One questioning activity for different purposes and outcomes.

Ash is looking to develop students' questioning skills in general. Jody is aiming for students to develop inquiry questions specifically. Casey is intending to stretch student thinking during a unit on space exploration.

The three teachers all begin by showing the students a few visuals related to the Mars One colony and by providing them with a few important background facts about the Mars One mission.

The table on the next pages summarizes for each of the three teachers, the goals of the questioning activity, the possible instructions and prompts the teacher may use, and examples of possible student questions, feedback and next steps.

FIGURE 3.9 Photos and images can be a powerful way of stimulating wonder and questions. What might students ask after seeing these images? Source: Mars One and Bryan Versteeg

THINQ

- How does this case study stretch your thinking on the purposes of and opportunities for student questioning?

- How could you use a provocation such as the Mars One mission to get your students asking questions?

- What methods (e.g., practice, modeling, feedback, anchor charts, self-assessment) do you use to improve your students' questioning skills?

- How do you get students to stretch their questioning to include different perspectives and purposes?

Teacher	Activity goal	Instructions for students	Sample student questions
Ash's activity	For students to generate different types of questions, from different perspectives and for different purposes.	• Look at the images of the proposed Mars One mission • Individually, write as many questions as you can about the Mars One mission on separate post-its (the teacher may consider a specific time-limit). • Individually, consider your questions and think of ways they might be grouped based on similarities. • Together in your inquiry group, discuss your questions and make categories for all of them.	Factual questions: • How will you breathe on Mars? • Why would anyone want to go there? • What will they eat? • Are there Martians there? • What's the point of going to Mars? • Are you going to die there?
Jody's activity	To have students create inquiry questions based on the Mars One Mission.	• Look at the images of the proposed Mars One mission • Complete Reproducible 3C, *Student exploration: Asking questions arising from provocations* individually and then in collaborative inquiry groups.	Student inquiry questions: • Is it possible to live on Mars? • Is it worth going to Mars? • Will human life be better on Mars? • What do we hope to achieve by going to Mars? • Who is best suited for life on Mars? • What are the limits of space exploration?
Casey's activity	To have students consider key scientific concepts and theories, questions and disciplinary thinking in a unit on space exploration.	• Individually, ask as many questions as you can about the Mars One mission. Be sure to show in your questions your understanding of the theories of space and scientific and technology concepts that we have previously explored.	• What technological tools and devices will be needed in the spacecraft? • How will the mission cope with dust storms? • What hemisphere of Mars are they going to? • What life support systems will be required? • Is it possible to create a human colony on Mars? • How much energy will it take to get a spacecraft to Mars (as compared to the Moon)? • How much time will it take? • What might it cost? • Who would be best suited for the colonization of Mars? • Should we colonize Mars?

Sample teacher prompts	Sample teacher feedback	Next steps
• What questions do you have? • How could you/did you categorize your questions? • Did you consider asking questions about (insert important concept here)? • Which questions do you most wish to answer? Why? • Where could you find the answer? • Are some of these questions easier to answer than others? Why? • What did you learn from listening to each other's questions? What questions were the same? Which ones were different? • How could we get better at asking questions?	• Great questions; you are curious and looking at the mission from different perspectives such as personal survival, group norms, ethics, and economics. • You asked great questions from the perspective of personal survival. Now try to think about the mission from the perspective of: a scientist, a person who wants to go on the mission, potential Martian lifeforms. • You are listening well to each other's questions. Now try to build on and improve each other's questions by making them clear, interesting and relevant to the topic of space travel.	• If students are asking only a few questions, consider modeling one question from a different perspective or for a different purpose and then allowing them to create additional ones with a partner. • Students or groups of students choose a question to answer and share their finding with the class.
• What are you feeling when you look at these images? • What are you thinking when you look at these images? • Can you think about this issue ethically (what is right and wrong)? • Do your inquiry questions require justification and not just an answer? • Do your questions invite me to think and not just "search" for the answer?	• This is a great inquiry question; it requires reasoning to answer and not just a simple Internet search. • This is a great inquiry question; it has come from your genuine curiosity and confusion about the mission. • Did someone in your group create an inquiry question that made you think about something in a way you never considered before? • This question is not an inquiry question. Which of the criteria do you think it does not meet? How could you revise it?	• Students or groups of students choose an inquiry question to answer. They begin to brainstorm other important questions they must first answer in order to be able to justify an answer to the inquiry question.
• We discussed many of the hazards of space travel, can you include them specifically in a question? • We have talked about current spacecraft, what questions might you have about this specific space mission? • What key features of Mars that we learned about will most impact this mission? • What did you learn from listening to each other's questions? What questions were the same? Which ones were different? • How could we get better at asking questions?	• Your questions show that you understand how spacecraft work. • Your questions show that you are thinking about the technology required to get to Mars. Can you add some questions about living in a colony on Mars? • Your questions need to show that you understand some of the mathematics involved in getting a spacecraft to Mars.	• As a whole class, examine the questions and account for how many questions require an understanding of important scientific concepts of the space unit (e.g., solar system, environment, technology, orbits, gravity, velocity) and build on the questions, if required. • Students or groups of students select questions to answer.

3.4 What questions can help student inquiry thinking?

Inquiry-based learning requires considerable amounts of reasoning which may pose challenges for many junior students. We can't just ask students to "think harder" — we need to describe exactly what good thinking involves and encourage students to be attentive to their own thinking, even when we are not there prompting them to do so. Analytical questions can assist an inquiry learner to "think about their thinking" and to improve thinking.

In their work on critical thinking, Paul and Elder (2010) identify eight universal elements that can be used to analyze and improve thinking (see Figure 3.10). These elements of thought are the springboard of the analytical questions provided in Figure 3.11. These analytical questions break down thinking (either a learner's thinking or the thinking inferred from evidence) into discrete parts that can be carefully examined.

Analytical questions based on the eight elements of thought will be helpful to your students during an inquiry. These questions can guide students and can also be used as important assessment information to help students improve their thinking. You could consider using some of these analytical questions in students' portfolio work and conferencing.

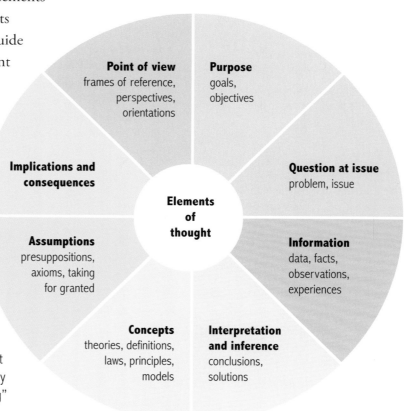

FIGURE 3.10 Focusing on different ways of thinking can assist an inquiry learner to "think about their thinking" and to improve it.

Questions to unpack and inquiry	
Questions to begin and unpack an inquiry	• Why do we care about this issue? • What do we hope to find out? • How will we proceed to answer the question/solve the problem? • What are my questions?
Questions that unpack concepts (concepts are an idea of what something is or how it works)	• What is the main idea you are using in your thinking? • Can you explain the concept (the idea) to me? • Is there a different concept that would work in considering this problem?
Questions that unpack working with "what is currently known"	• What is the source of this information? • What is the quality of this information? • How am I making meaning of this information? • What does the author or speaker take for granted? • What am I taking for granted? • What alternative beliefs are there to consider? • What are the relevant points of view? • What is my point of view? • Can I explain my thinking as I summarize, synthesize and assess this evidence? • What am I finding difficult, and what steps could I take?
Questions that unpack reaching a conclusion or "putting it all together"	• Do I have all the information I need? • How did I reach my conclusion? How did I solve the problem? • Have I considered other alternative and plausible conclusions/solutions? • Where is this argument/conclusion/point of view leading us? • What will happen if my conclusion is correct?

FIGURE 3.11 Asking questions is a powerful way to guide students towards a successful conclusion to their inquiry.

THINQ

• Which of the eight elements of thought do your students typically use?

• Which of the eight elements of thought do you need to introduce to your students?

• Thinking back to the importance of triangulated assessment evidence, what evidence of student learning could you use to assess student responses to the questions above?

3.5 How can I assess students as they ask questions?

Chapter 2 provided some assessment strategies to help you gather evidence of student learning during an inquiry. In that chapter, we suggest that the six essential abilities of inquiry learners be at the core of inquiry activities and inquiry assessment. Questioning is a crucial skill of inquiry and is found in each method of inquiry and each stage of every model. For example, a student cannot "understand what is currently know" if they do not ask questions of sources and ideas. "Thinking together" cannot happen without students respectfully asking each other, and themselves, to identify beliefs and inferences and to explain reasoning. Students obviously cannot demonstrate curiosity without being able to voice their questions.

Reproducible 3E, *Assessment planning template: Asks questions* can be used to plan your triangulated assessment evidence collection. Reproducible 3F, *Inquiry rubric and self-check: Asks questions* can be used by teachers and students to assess and evaluate the skill of questioning as found in each of the six essential abilities of inquiry learners. Keep in mind that you do not have to use every criteria in the rubric, only those that apply your inquiry and questioning activities.

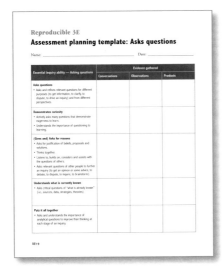
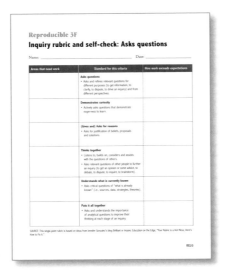

FIGURE 3.12 Reproducible 3E, p. RE19.   **FIGURE 3.13** Reproducible 3F, p. RE20.

INQUIRY FOR ALL

Questioning games

Questioning games help build the skills of the junior learner and allow them to take risks while having fun.

1. **Mystery Bag:** Create a modified "show and tell" by bringing something to school that can be put in a bag. Other students must guess what's inside.

2. **Why/What if/How Game:** Introduce an interesting and relevant problem. Have students use the Why/What if/How? format to ask as many questions they can in a two minute time frame.

3. **Dice Game:** Assign each digit on a dice a topic (e.g., friends, science, sports). Also assign each digit a question starter (e.g., what, when, why, how, who, where). Students roll the dice and create questions. How many questions can be created in one minute with multiple rolls of the dice?

4. **"Ask an Intelligent Assistant":** Students create humorous and serious questions for artificial intelligence interfaces (e.g. "Siri" for Apple).

Can or should I level student questions?

It may be tempting to level or assess students' questions based on charts showing various combinations of the parts of speech such as the one in Figure 3.14, but we advise against this practice. Students should create questions for various purposes and recognize the purpose of questions. For example, "How big is Mars?" is an excellent question aimed at gathering information. The question "Why would we want to go to Mars?" is another excellent question that asks for evaluation of information. Students require practice and modelling to extend their repertoire of questions based on different purposes.

Learners need to ask all types of question during an inquiry, yet many of them would be considered "low level" by some questioning assessment tools. But it is very difficult to interpret the complexity of many questions based on parts of speech. What we need to consider instead, is the learner's purpose and the thinking behind their question. For example, the question "When is it acceptable to fight?" or "Is war wrong?" may be scored as a low questions when in fact these questions meet all the criteria of a deep inquiry question. It is important to keep in mind that all questions that move the inquiry along are important; from the information gathering "factual" questions to synthesis, application and evaluative questions as in Figure 3.15.

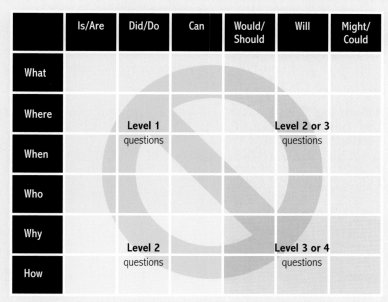

	Is/Are	Did/Do	Can	Would/Should	Will	Might/Could
What						
Where		Level 1			Level 2 or 3	
When		questions			questions	
Who						
Why		Level 2			Level 3 or 4	
How		questions			questions	

FIGURE 3.14 It may be tempting to assess questions using a table such as this one. However, it's quite possible a student could generate a Level 4 "Who is" question as well as a Level 1 "How might" question.

	Is/Are	Did/Do	Can	Would/Should	Will	Might/Could
What						
Where		Factual			Predictive	
When		questions			questions	
Who						
Why		Analytical			Application Synthesis	
How		questions			questions	

FIGURE 3.15 Questioning charts provide a visual anchor for students who need support in extending the types of questions they are asking. Avoid placing a value on or judging students questions prematurely.

Revisit and reflect

This chapter looked closely at the importance of wonder and curiosity to initiate and sustain inquiry learning. A classroom culture that encourages curiosity, risk-taking, open-mindedness and persistence fosters wonder and the resulting questions.

We outlined the importance of creating powerful inquiry questions that can capture and hold student interest and propel their learning. Wonder activities and provocations were offered as ways to promote questioning. Analytical questions were detailed that can help students distinguish "weak" thinking from "strong" thinking in both themselves and others.

THINQ

- To conclude your exploration of this chapter, take some time to complete Reproducible 3G, *Teacher checklist: Curiosity and questions in my classroom.*

BIG IDEAS

3.1 Our curiosity fuels our learning.

3.2 The purpose of an inquiry question is to entice students to think deeply about the mysteries of life.

3.3 Questions that elicit strong emotions are the best place to begin.

3.4 We need to describe exactly what good thinking involves and encourage students to be attentive to their own thinking.

3.5 Teachers need to help students become better questioners.

Reproducible 3G

Teacher checklist: Curiosity and questions in my classroom

Check which of the following statements represents your teaching practice. The focus of this checklist is questioning, an essential quality of inquiry thinking. Use this checklist for self-reflection, planning and sharing with colleagues, and to determine next steps in deepening inquiry practice.

- Students' questions are taken up in meaningful ways in my classroom.
- Students get to practise asking different types of questions in my classroom.
- Students understand why asking questions is important to learning in general, and inquiry learning in particular.
- Students in my classroom know there are different types of questions with different purposes and apply this knowledge.
- Students pose questions (including inquiry questions) and real world problems that relate to their lives and the "real world."
- Students ask analytical questions of their thinking during an inquiry.
- Students understand the criteria for effective questioning and can effectively self- and peer-assess questions.
- I use a variety of provocations to pique and sustain student curiosity, wonder and questioning.
- I pose questions and/or real world problems that relate to students' lives and the "real world."
- I pose questions and/or real world problems to provoke student curiosity and accelerate students' desire to learn.
- I organize factual knowledge around conceptual frameworks and open-ended inquiry questions to facilitate knowledge retrieval and application.
- I pose analytical questions to help students improve their thinking.
- I pose instructional questions to reveal students' prior knowledge, including preconceptions and misconceptions regarding important concepts.
- I assess students' questioning abilities through conversations, observations and products.

RE21

FIGURE 3.16 Reproducible 3G, p. RE21.

Chapter 4
INVESTIGATING AND EXPLORING:
Finding answers to inquiry questions

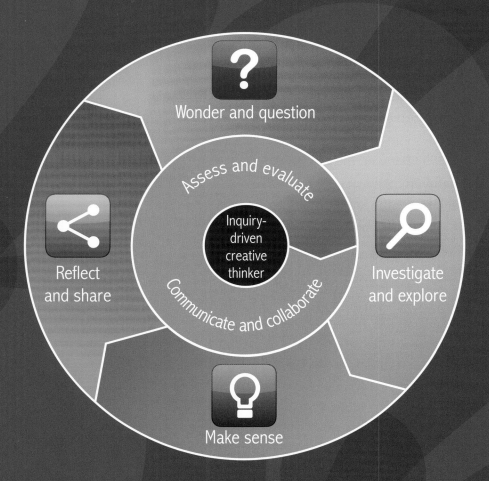

Wonder and question

Assess and evaluate

Inquiry-driven creative thinker

Reflect and share

Communicate and collaborate

Investigate and explore

Make sense

4.1 How do I get my students interested in finding answers to their questions?

Some teachers tell us the process of developing inquiry questions is engaging for students — and for themselves — but that the fun stops once it's time to gather and organize evidence. We think this may be because this stage of inquiry often defaults to a traditional research process: a student is given a topic, they go to the library to do research and then typically prepare a written research report. But this isn't what the gather and organize stage has to look like.

We have deliberately called this chapter and this stage of the inquiry process *investigating and exploring* because we want to signal the fact that this is an active, interesting and often exciting phase of inquiry. This is where students get to explore and examine information in their search for answers to their questions. This process of investigation occurs whether you, the teacher, provide the information for students, students conduct research and locate the information for themselves, or some combination of both.

Creating an investigative mindset

The key to making this stage engaging for you and your students is to treat the process as being all about exploration. This is their chance to solve the "problem" of their question. Since this stage of the inquiry process is very important, we believe it is worth taking the time to make it fun and engaging for students. After all, if we are

TEACHER QUERIES

What do I do when students always expect ME to answer their questions?

Many teachers tell us that they want to create a classroom rooted in investigation and exploration, but that they "get stuck" when their students look to them — the teacher — to answer their questions for them. It's true that students are used to teachers always answering their questions. Many know if they wait long enough, the teacher will provide an answer.

Teachers who are confident in an inquiry-based classroom do not rescue students when they initially request an answer. Data shows that, more often than not, the student actually understands more than they initially demonstrate. When given the encouragement to think in a safe learning environment students actually develop the skills to persevere and trust their thinking abilities. It's important to resist the temptation to always respond, even if you know the answer. If we want students to think for themselves, then we need to let them think for themselves.

If you want to foster an investigative mindset the next time your students push you for an answer, try responding with a question:

- "That's an interesting question! Where might you find the answer to that?"

- "I've never thought about that! Let's find out together. Where should we look first?"

- "This is a new topic for me and I don't know the answer. Please come and share with me when you find something about that."

trying to change the way students learn by putting them more in charge their learning, then we have to shake up the way they have traditionally gathered and processed information.

Everyone, but especially junior learners, love to solve puzzles and problems. By creating a classroom that puts students in the role of knowledge seekers or problems solvers, student engagement and interest increases.

There are a number of ways we can let our students know that our classroom is a place of investigation and exploration, such as the examples in Figure 4.1. These ideas send the message that your classroom is an *active learning environment*: one where exploration and discovery are the norm.

Activities to create an investigative classroom

- **Place an "Open for Learning" sign** on your door with the word "business" crossed out and replaced with the word "learning" (see Reproducible 4A).

- **Hand out props and nametags** to students, such as lab coats or "Mad Scientist" labels so that they can be "scientists" for the day. If you are doing history, you could print up "explorer" labels.

- **Create mystery boxes** by placing large question marks on shoe boxes, or an assortment of boxes in different sizes. Inside put photos, objects or art that will act as clues or provocations for the day's lesson.

- **Make predictions posters** to place around your room. These posters could contain images where something is about to happen (e.g., a person climbing a tall ladder), with three possible outcomes listed below. Students can guess which one they believe will occur.

- **Do a countdown** to the moment when you send students off to find solutions and answers, to create a sense of anticipation. You can ring a bell, wave a flag, or simply count down from five.

FIGURE 4.1 You can send a message that your classroom is an active learning environment: one where exploration and discovery are the norm.

Reproducible 4A
"Open for learning" sign

OPEN for business learning!

RE22

FIGURE 4.2 Reproducible 4A, p. RE22.

4.2 What is the role of the teacher during the investigation stage of an inquiry?

In our work with teachers, a common question we hear is, "What is my role in helping students to *answer* the inquiry question?" Broadly speaking, teachers need to be both leaders — to guide and support students through the learning process — and co-learners, exploring new content and ideas alongside their students. However, we are sure that we frustrate teachers when we also say "it depends." In the same way that there is no "right" answer to an inquiry question, there is no one answer about a teacher's role. We say "it depends" because the role of the teacher during the actual inquiry is dependent on a number of considerations. These include: the ages and abilities of the students in the class; the students' previous experience with research; whether or not students have access to technology in the classroom or library; how much time teachers have allotted to the inquiry in their planning; and the teacher's goals for this stage of the inquiry. Figure 4.3 may help you to determine the role you will play during the inquiry.

As you can see in Figure 4.3, if many of your students are not yet independent readers, do not have a great deal of research experience, and if Wi-Fi access in your classroom or library is unreliable, then this phase of the inquiry will probably need to be teacher-directed. It is worth noting that the role you play in one particular inquiry may not be the same as the role you will play in subsequent inquiries. As your students gain more experience with inquiry and develop specific inquiry skills, and as you gain more experience facilitating inquiry-based learning, your role will naturally evolve to meet the unique needs of your students from year to year.

More teacher direction	Determining your role during the investigative stage of an inquiry	Less teacher direction
Very little	Do my students have experience gathering and organizing evidence?	Quite a lot
Not yet	Are my students independent readers?	Pretty much
Not much	Do my students have experience doing research online?	Quite a lot
Not really	Do my students have convenient and reliable access to the Internet or library?	Yes absolutely
Very little	How much time do I have for this stage of the inquiry?	Quite a lot

FIGURE 4.3 Your role in an inquiry will depend upon the skills and experiences of your students and the conditions in your classroom.

4.3 How should I facilitate the investigation stage of an inquiry?

An inquiry can sometimes falter at the point where students have to develop answers to their questions. There are a number of reasons why this may be the case:

- Some students like to be told the answers by the teacher, rather than developing an answer for themselves.

- Learning something new is hard work.

- Making sense of conflicting information is difficult.

- Sometimes students don't know how to navigate themselves around a "dead end" during the inquiry process.

In this section, we will highlight ways to address these considerations.

Planning for preconceptions and misconceptions

Students don't come to our classrooms as empty vessels waiting to be filled up. They arrive with a host of prior knowledge and experiences. Students process new information *through* those experiences, beliefs and understandings — as do we! This is neither bad nor good, but it is important to be aware of and plan for, so we can manage its impact during inquiry.

Prior knowledge and experiences interact in our brain and result in preconceptions (ideas and opinions formed ahead of time) or misconceptions (false beliefs or notions) about certain topics, issues or ideas. We can mitigate the impact that preconceptions and misconceptions have on the acquisition of new knowledge by helping students identify their currently held beliefs at each stage of an inquiry.

Preconceptions and misconceptions affect inquiry because students will likely give greater weight to evidence that supports their currently held beliefs than evidence that challenges them. In their book *Intentional Interruption* (2013), Steven Katz and Lisa Ain Dack call this mental barrier a *confirmation bias.* Katz and Dack make the case that people of all ages — from very young children to adults — work hard to avoid evidence that challenges what they already think, believe, know and do.

As well, if students are conducting their own research, personal point of view may impact the types of evidence searches they conduct. That is, students may not be able to consider the multiple ways that an inquiry question can be answered because they already hold a preconception about the question under investigation.

To help junior students uncover their preconceptions and misconceptions, you can walk them through a simple exercise that asks them to consider their currently held beliefs and ideas about the inquiry topic (see Reproducible 3D, *What I see, what I think, what I wonder, what I feel,* p. RE18). Junior-aged students can learn to stop and consider what they see, think, wonder and feel about a topic before they begin further exploration. This should help them keep an open-mind as they acquire new knowledge. The first time you ask students to conduct this analysis, you should model the completion of the reproducible with the entire class. Walk them through a topic they all have some knowledge about, and complete the reproducible as a group.

The reflective prompt "What do I already know or think about this question?" is an important starting point in inquiry-based learning because it sends the message that students themselves are "knowledge keepers." In school, we do not often treat students as if they are knowledgeable and can contribute to the development of a response to a question. We turn to books, the internet, videos and "experts" for answers to the questions we pose in our classrooms. If we want students to see themselves as active participants in their learning, and believe they have something valuable and meaningful to say, we need to recognize their own experience and knowledge in relation to the questions we ask.

Locating grade and age-appropriate sources

Whether you provide your students with the information they require to conduct their inquiry or have them conduct their own research, there are a number of non-negotiables during the investigation phase of an inquiry. One of these is that junior learners must work from grade- and age-appropriate sources.

If your students will be working from print sources, make sure that the print sources you provide (or direct your students to read) are actually readable. This might sound obvious, but it is often easier said than done.

INQUIRY FOR ALL

Identifying preconceptions

It is important that all students conduct this preliminary critical thinking exercise (Reproducible 3D). Students who have trouble completing a written learning journal should have the option of recording their information using a mobile or assistive device, or working with a helper to capture their learning. As well, some students may require a conversation with you to successfully navigate this exercise. This provides you with a great opportunity to have one-on-one time with specific students.

CAPACITY
What are some of the obstacles you face in finding and/or creating age-appropriate inquiry resources?

COMMITMENT
Does the need to find and possibly adapt age-appropriate, multi-perspective source materials shake your commitment to do more inquiry?

Most print resources accessed with a simple Internet search will be at a language level above most junior learners. If you preview the print sources you will know whether you have to pre-teach specific vocabulary or provide background information to make the readings comprehensible.

As well, if print sources are too long, students will disengage or turn off before they even begin the reading process. With junior learners we recommend making drastic edits to the length of print sources. Younger students are much more willing to read many small pieces or snippets of information about a topic than two or three longer pieces.

The same rules apply to video or audio sources. Shorter video or audio clips are always better than longer ones. Although a commonly held belief is that students can focus their attention in a concentrated way for 10–15 minutes, more recent research suggests the period of focused attention is closer to 4.5 to 5 minutes at a time (Dufault, 2013). As well, video segments that involve animation or some type of action, rather than talking heads, are more engaging for students.

Remember that you don't have to deliver "information" to junior learners through print and video only. In fact, if you can deliver the same content to students through photographs, artwork, and objects, this will likely be more engaging and accessible for most of your students. This has the added bonus of allowing students to work directly from primary sources.

Considering multiple perspectives

When any student searches for an answer to an inquiry question, we always want them to look for and consider multiple points of view. In fact, when we think about big ideas or enduring understandings — the things that students will remember long after a course or period of learning has concluded — the automatic consideration of multiple points of view is, for us, of vital importance.

We want our students to learn not to rush to judgment. In a world where we have unlimited access to information, this is one

---

TECH-ENABLED INQUIRY

Searching the Internet

While junior learners may be regular users of mobile technologies, they may not be familiar with what the Internet is, how it works or how to use it effectively to find answers to their inquiry questions.

Understand what your students can do in this regard and close the gaps on the basics of effective internet searches. Model a basic search with the whole class:

1. Define the purpose of the search.

2. Choose a search engine (there are many engines designed for kids such as Google Junior, KidzSearch or KidRex).

3. Choose a keyword, search and review the results.

4. Choose a second keyword and link them with Boolean operators (and, or, not) to refine the results.

5. Evaluate the quality of the sources (see Reproducible 4B or 4C on pp. RE23–RE24).

of *the* most important critical thinking skills this generation of students needs.

This is key, not only intellectually, but also from the perspective of citizenship. Our students are growing up in a diverse, globally connected world. No child, regardless of where they live, will be isolated from this 21st century reality. Therefore, students, even very young students, must be exposed to the idea that there are many different and often conflicting perspectives on any issue. They should understand that they need to seriously consider and respect these different points of view before coming to their own conclusions. In the end, we want their best considered response, with the understanding that there is always more to think about well beyond the learning period timeframe.

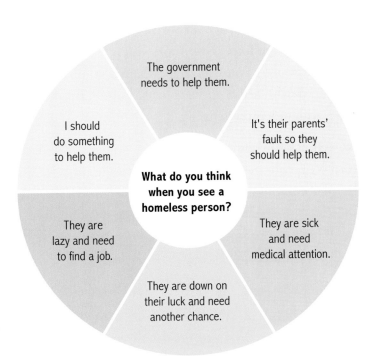

FIGURE 4.4 An inquiry around homelessness should surface many different perspectives about the possible causes and solutions.

At its most basic level, this means ensuring that the information students consider — whether located by themselves or provided by you — meets the following criteria:

- the resources include at least two, but preferably three or more different points of view or conflicting pieces of information.

- the information includes samples from mainstream media (e.g., national broadcaster, national paper, or government publication/website) and alternative media (e.g., small independent news agencies, independent documentary companies, credible bloggers, voices outside the mainstream).

- the information includes at least one position in support of and one position against the issue under exploration.

We realize that if you are gathering resource material for your students, time is an issue. However, as teachers it is important that we promote the idea that issues are not black and white. If time is an issue we recommend doing a smaller number of rich inquiries that explore an issue in depth and reflect multiple perspectives, rather than numerous inquiries that do not dig as deeply.

Determining the quality of sources

While you may choose to provide packages of source information for your younger students or for students who do not have much experience with research, at some point you will want to release the responsibility for gathering information to your students.

Students should consider three key questions about the credibility and usefulness of their information as evidence:

- **Source:** Who wrote it and what makes the person an authority or expert on this topic?
- **Purpose:** For what purpose was it created? Was it created to influence people? Was it created to promote a product and make money?
- **Support:** Is it supported by other evidence? Can you find other evidence that supports this data or point of view? If not, why not?

Tools for evaluating sources and evidence

There are many tools you can use to help your students think about the quality and usefulness of the information they find. Here are two examples.

P.A.S.S. (See Reproducible 4B, *Evaluating sources and evidence: P.A.S.S.*)

- **Purpose:** Why and when was it created?
- **Accuracy:** Is the information current, truthful and unbiased?
- **Source:** Who created it? Are they an expert?
- **Support:** Is it supported by other information and sources?

U.S.E. I.T. (See Reproducible 4C, *Evaluating sources and evidence: U.S.E. I.T.*)

- **Usefulness:** Does it help me answer the question?
- **Source:** Who created it and why?
- **Evidence:** Is it supported by other evidence?
- **Impartial:** Is it fair and unbiased?
- **Thinking:** Does it change my thinking?

FIGURE 4.5 You can introduce your students to frameworks for thinking about the quality of their sources and information, and how this can help them find answers and solutions.

Reproducible 4B

Evaluating sources and evidence: P.A.S.S.

Name: ______ Date: ______

Inquiry focus: ______

Evidence being evaluated: ______

Key questions		My evaluation of the evidence
P	PURPOSE Why and when was it created? Is it important to my inquiry?	
A	ACCURACY Is the information correct, truthful and unbiased? Should I use it?	
S	SOURCE Who created it? Are they an expert? Are they believable?	
S	SUPPORT Is it supported by other information and sources? What does this tell me?	

RE23

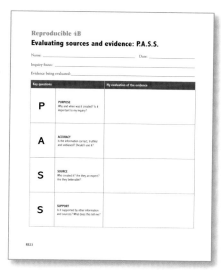

FIGURE 4.6 Reproducible 4B, p. RE23.

Reproducible 4C

Evaluating sources and evidence: U.S.E. I.T.

Name: ______ Date: ______

Inquiry focus: ______

Evidence being evaluated: ______

Key questions		My evaluation of the evidence
U	USEFULNESS How will it help me answer my question? How important is it?	
S	SOURCE Where did it come from? When was it created? Is it the original or has it been changed?	
E	EVIDENCE Is it supported by other evidence? What does it tell me?	
I	IMPARTIAL Is it fair and unbiased? Who created it? Why did they create it?	
T	THINKING Does it change my thinking? What does it tell me?	

Adapted from work developed by Jesse Denison and David Nolan during the York University certificate course in Inquiry-Based Learning (Spring 2015)

RE24

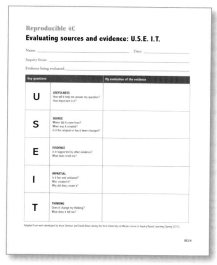

FIGURE 4.7 Reproducible 4C, p. RE24.

Building inquiry evidence bundles

In Canada, each province and territory has a number of history or social studies curriculum expectations targeting key social, economic and political developments in the country and their impact on members of First Nations, Métis and Inuit communities. (In Canada, members of First Nations, Métis and Inuit are also referred to as "indigenous peoples." Indigenous peoples are the earliest inhabitants of a geographic area or country.) There are also curriculum expectations that target personal identity and Canadian identity. Under the umbrella of the inquiry question, "How did government policies impact the identity of Indigenous Peoples?" we decided to address both of these broad curriculum expectations by focusing on the Canadian government's use of "Eskimo identification discs" to collect statistical data about the Inuit from the 1940s to the late 1960s.

Evidence bundle elements

This evidence bundle consists of the following elements:

- Figure 4.8 and 4.9: Two photos with captions removed.
- Figure 4.10 and 4.11: Two photo captions.
- Figure 4.12: An adapted excerpt from the Aboriginal Affairs and Northern Development Canada website.
- Figure 4.13: An excerpt from a story from *Nunatsiaq News*, an Iqaluit newspaper.

FIGURE 4.8

Photo caption: "Non-indigenous government agents had trouble with Inuit names and naming traditions so government agents classified people according to assigned numbers rather than actual names."

FIGURE 4.10

Photo caption: Kuujjuaq woman Olivia Ikey Duncan shows off her new tattoo, a depiction of the Eskimo identification discs issued to Canadian Inuit in the 1940s.

FIGURE 4.11

FIGURE 4.9

Excerpt 1: Adapted from Sarah Bonesteel, *Canada's Relationship with Inuit: A History of Policy and Program Development.* Aboriginal Affairs and Northern Development Canada, 2006.

Traditionally, Inuit names could be used for both boys and girls. Children were often named after dead family members, regardless of their sex. Inuit communities were small and so they only used one name and did not need to use last names or family names. In their oral culture, it was not necessary to write down a person's name or important to spell it the same way every time.

In some communities, Christian missionaries gave the Inuit biblical names from the Christian bible. These English names were not familiar to Inuit and often hard to say, so they sometimes altered them to make them easier to pronounce. Although Inuit were often known by these names within their communities, they also kept their Inuit names.

All of these different names, spellings and pronunciations did not seem to confuse the Inuit, but did confuse the non-Inuit persons who lived in Inuit communities. They found it very hard to pronounce and spell Inuit names. For example, Canadian government officials, police and doctors found it difficult to keep records of the Inuit because there were so many names, pronunciations and spellings.

In 1941, the Canadian government introduced an identification system to help them more easily identify and track the Inuit. Every Inuit was given a disc stamped with a four-digit number. The Canadian government kept a record of Inuit and Christian names, along with the disc number, or E [*Eskimo*]-number, given to each Inuk. The discs were approximately the size of a quarter with a hole punched in the top, so they could be worn on string around the neck or wrist. They were made from pressed fibre and stamped with the Canadian Coat of Arms as well as the four-digit number.

FIGURE 4.12

Excerpt 2: Sarah Rogers, "Kuujjuaq woman brings back symbol of the Inuit past", *Nunatsiaq News*, December 4, 2013.

KUUJJUAQ — The Eskimo identification discs once used by the Canadian government to track Inuit faded in the early 1970s as Inuit across the country adopted [last names].

But a young Nunavik woman has revived that symbol to tell a part of her history.

The inside of Olivia Ikey Duncan's right arm tells a story about her family's past: that's where she bears a tattoo of the coin-shaped disc, held in place by a thinly-inked string. "I always wanted a tattoo," said Duncan, 24. "But I didn't want a butterfly or a star, and I wanted it to say something about who I am."

Earlier this year, Duncan, who lives in Kuujjuaq, ... learned about [the identification discs and] and how Inuit and other groups were colonized.

"I cried so much that day — I couldn't believe that my people had gone through that and survived," she said. "How they were categorized, and how they were treated... that's when I said 'that's my tattoo.'"

... Before she decided on her tattoo, Duncan researched the history of the tags, and how Inuit were administered — a history she wishes was more available to Inuit youth today.

For Duncan, that part of her family's history seems so close — yet so far away for a generation, like hers, who grew up without them.

But people are trying to understand now and they want their discs back, to keep as a part of our history," she added.

"How can you be proud of yourself when you don't understand where you came from?"

FIGURE 4.13

Evidence bundle analysis

In this bundle we made sure to include a variety of materials: photos, captions and readings. The readings have been adapted for a younger student audience. You can view the original sources to see how they were altered. We included two perspectives on the identification discs: the federal government perspective, and the personal perspective of one Inuk woman.

You could build out this evidence bundle by adding materials such as maps, objects, art or videos, or by presenting more perspectives on this issue. You could also support your students as they look for additional materials, including discussions with guest speakers or Skype sessions with experts in the field. We chose to limit the amount of information in the bundle so that you could see that you can build a rich evidence bundle, representing more than one perspective, without dozens of materials.

Using this evidence bundle – "peeling the onion"

There are many possible ways to use evidence bundles. One method we have found effective is to distribute items to groups of students one at a time, asking them to record their questions about the piece of evidence they are examining. As you release additional items, they can add new questions to their list. We think of this gradual release of information as peeling an onion. There are a number of benefits to releasing information in this manner:

- Students feel like they are detectives solving a mystery. With this approach we have seen high levels of engagement in students of all ages, including adults!

- You should release the most accessible source material first. That is, the source material that is the easiest to read or process. In our experience this is often photographs and objects. So with this bundle, we would first distribute one photo, wait a few minutes and then distribute the second photo and so on.

- The gradual release of information reduces the chances that students become overwhelmed by an entire source package that may seem too big or challenging.

- Students can see how their questions change and deepen as they examine new evidence. In a perfect world, eventually we'd like students to internalize why relying on a single piece of evidence can lead to weak questions and flawed conclusions.

When the student groups have all of the evidence, you could ask them to review their entire list of questions and settle on one or two they would like to explore further. Or, you could have them share their questions and generate a master list for the class. As a class you could then develop an overarching inquiry question that links back to the high-level curriculum expectations, and four or five sub-inquiry questions for investigation by student groups.

THINQ

- What types of source evidence do your students find the easiest to process?

- How can you build upon the types of evidence students are exposed to?

- Do you generally release source evidence to your students piece by piece in a scaffolded way? What might be the advantages and disadvantages of doing so?

4.4 How do I assess the investigation phase of the inquiry process?

Chapter 2, *Assessing and evaluating* provided some assessment strategies to help you gather evidence of student learning during an inquiry. In that chapter, we suggest that the six essential abilities of inquiry learners are at the core of inquiry activities and inquiry assessment. Those essential abilities are key during the investigation phase of an inquiry as well.

Investigating the inquiry question is a crucial part of the inquiry process. In this chapter we have suggested that teachers gather and organize rich, age-appropriate evidence bundles for their students, or at least gather and organize a portion of the evidence to facilitate student success at this stage of the inquiry.

Reproducible 4D, *Assessment planning template: Understands what is currently known* can be used to plan your triangulated assessment evidence collection. Reproducible 4E, *Inquiry rubric and self-check: Understands what is currently known* can be used as a guide by you and your students to assess and evaluate the skills of investigation as found in each of the six essential abilities of inquiry learners.

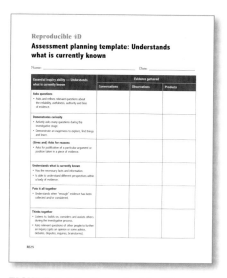

FIGURE 4.14 Reproducible 4D, p. RE25.

THINQ

- How do you currently assess the investigation phase of the inquiry process?

- Is this an area in which you feel proficient, or do you feel you would benefit from further professional learning on this aspect of inquiry?

- Where might you be able to inject more assessment *for* learning into class time devoted to the investigation phase of the inquiry process?

- What would be the benefits of doing so?

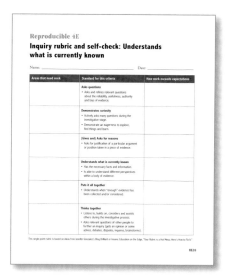

FIGURE 4.15 Reproducible 4E, p. RE26.

Revisit and reflect

In this chapter we argued that teachers can foster an investigative mindset that sees problems and questions as challenges, and views the search for answers as interesting and exciting.

We explored how teachers can assist students with the investigative process, including:

- the need to foster an investigative mindset,

- how to create classroom conditions that encourage an investigative mindset, and

- working from a set of criteria for a rich and balanced investigation.

We examined how source evidence can be prepared and shared with students and concluded by reviewing a number of assessment tools designed to measure students' abilities to navigate the investigative phase of the inquiry process.

To conclude your exploration of this chapter, take some time to complete Reproducible 4F, *Teacher checklist: Investigative mindset in my classroom.*

THINQ

- What are one or two specific strategies you could implement in your classroom to signal to your students that your classroom is a place for investigation?

- How might your own confirmation biases influence the types of sources you introduce to your students?

- Do you prefer to have students find their own evidence to answer an inquiry question or to provide the information for your students? What are the advantages and disadvantages of both of these approaches?

- How might you improve how you integrate multiple points of view in response to the questions, issues or problems explored in your classroom?

- How can you improve your students' ability to assess the quality of sources and evidence?

BIG IDEAS

4.1 Students are more interested in searching for an "answer" to a question if they believe the teacher is eager to see what they can uncover.

4.2 To adopt an inquiry stance, teachers need to be both leaders and co-learners alongside their students.

4.3 Teachers need to model an inquiry stance as well as provide parameters and structures to ensure student success.

4.4 The ability to "understand what is currently known" is essential for the inquiry learner.

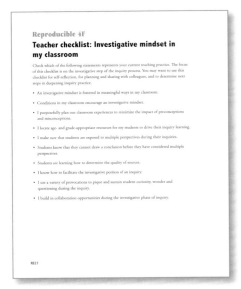

FIGURE 4.16 Reproducible 4F, p. RE27.

Chapter 5
MAKING SENSE:
Synthesizing and consolidating learning

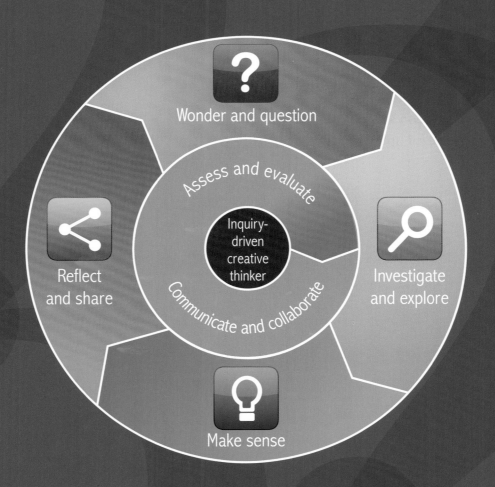

Wonder and question

Assess and evaluate

Inquiry-driven creative thinker

Reflect and share

Communicate and collaborate

Investigate and explore

Make sense

5.1 What do we mean when we ask students to "synthesize"?

One of the goals of inquiry — and indeed, the intended outcome of inquiry — is for students to create new knowledge. This happens naturally after students discover something they didn't previously know, reflect on what they have learned, and/or draw conclusions based on their learning.

The creation of new knowledge often, but not exclusively, comes after a body of evidence is synthesized or consolidated. Synthesis can be a complicated process, and just like other elements of learning, needs to be taught explicitly. As you will see in the feature "Words matter," many of the words used to describe the synthesis process are unfamiliar and likely confusing for young learners. We have chosen to call this chapter "making sense" because ultimately, that is really what students have to do at this stage of an inquiry: make sense of all the information and learning that has occurred up to this point.

FIGURE 5.1 The synthesis process allows us to make meaning out of seemingly disconnected pieces of information, data and evidence.

It doesn't matter whether we are working with junior learners, preschool learners or adult learners: learning something new is really hard. In their book *Intentional Interruption: Breaking Down Learning Barriers to Transform Professional Practice* (2013), Stephen Katz and Lisa Ain Dack remind us that there are a number of psychological barriers that hinder new learning for most individuals, as presented in Figure 5.2

If adults fall prey to these psychological barriers, it seems reasonable to assume that younger people do too. It's important for us, as teachers, to be aware of these psychological barriers to learning so we can help our students avoid them.

CONFIRMATION

Do you agree with Katz and Dack that real learning is hard? Does it reflect your own professional learning experiences?

Brain barriers to learning	
We find thinking hard. People really dislike hard thinking and therefore avoid it.	**We can't see all options.** People aren't very good at thinking through all possible options when making decisions.
Our thinking is biased. People tend to accept information and ideas that confirm what they already think, believe, know and do, and dismiss evidence to the contrary.	**We believe being wrong is weak.** People keep their questions to themselves because they believe not knowing or being wrong is seen as a weakness.

FIGURE 5.2 Human beings are flawed thinkers, and that can create barriers to learning.

THINQ

- In your experience, do junior learners find it difficult to synthesize or consolidate a body of evidence?

- Do you have strategies to assist your students with the synthesis process, or is this an area you would like to improve in your practice?

- Are there opportunities within your school for teachers to share effective strategies with one another? If not, could this be a great target for a future staff meeting?

WORDS MATTER

There are a number of words that refer to the synthesis process. You may want to post some or all of these words around your room under the heading "Making Sense."

Arrange
Move and organize into a particular order.

Assemble
Put or fit together.

Combine
Bring together or join into a whole.

Consolidate
Bring together into a single or unified whole.

Construct
Build or form by putting together the parts.

Integrate
Unite to make a whole or larger unit.

Make sense
Come to a logical explanation or understanding.

Synthesize
Make something new by combining different things.

5.2 What are some obstacles in the synthesis process?

As teachers, we often caution our students about the synthesis process. We tell students to make sure they consider all their evidence carefully, we tell them not to jump to conclusions, and we tell them to consider bias in the information they have collected. We certainly give the impression that "making sense" is a minefield of trouble!

But what we don't often do is explain why we are providing all these cautions. We don't actually explore with our students how the human brain works when processing information. And perhaps even more importantly, we don't explore the fact that our brains make "errors."

We feel that it is worthwhile exploring this phenomenon with junior learners so that they begin to have a better understanding of how their brains work. If students understand that the human brain makes errors when processing information, they may proceed more carefully when synthesizing and drawing conclusions.

Treating inferences as facts

One way that the human brain makes "errors" is by making inferences and then treating those inferences as facts. You can explore this phenomenon with your students by doing a few simple optical illusion experiments in class. We have provided a few images here to get you started, but you can use Google Images in your classroom for the same result. When we stare at each of the images below, our brains play tricks on us. Students will want to know how this happens!

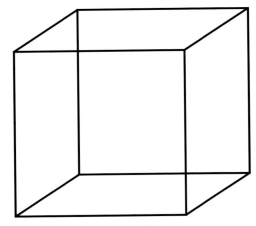

FIGURE 5.3 When you stare at this Necker Cube, the faces of the cube move forward and backward. This "brain error" occurs as a result of the fact that this is an ambiguous line drawing which does not include any depth cues.

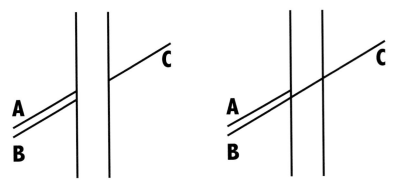

FIGURE 5.4 Look at this Poggendorff illusion. In the diagram on the left, can you tell which diagonal line connects: line A-C or line B-C? If you look at the diagram on the right, you can see that it's line B-C. This optical illusion is the result of the brain's misperception of the interaction between diagonal lines and horizontal and vertical edges.

FIGURE 5.5 The visual cues in this illusion make your brain think that the purple and green columns are moving and sinking into the space below.

Students know that these optical illusions don't make sense, but they also know that they see them! There is a scientific explanation for each of these illusions, which you can discuss with your students if you choose, but the big idea we want to emphasize is that our brains are constantly making inferences and drawing conclusions when processing information. Often the inference is correct, but sometimes it isn't. When our brains make an incorrect inference based on *visual* information, then an optical illusion is the result.

After doing a few optical illusions with your students, you may choose to broaden the discussion by exploring other phenomenon that result in brain errors: lack of sleep, hunger, poor nutrition and extremes of temperature, to name a few.

At the conclusion of this exploration you'll want to make an explicit connection back to the issue at hand: the synthesis of new information. In particular, if the human brain can make errors processing "factual" visual information, then of course the brain can make errors while trying to make sense of new information.

FOOD FOR THOUGHT

"There are two ways to be fooled. One is to believe what isn't true. The other is to refuse to accept what is true."
Soren Kierkegaard

Confirmation bias

The human brain has a tendency to search for or interpret information in a way that confirms what a person already believes. Psychologists call this a confirmation bias, and it can impact the synthesis stage of the inquiry process. Once a person has gathered a body of evidence, humans usually actively seek out and assign more weight to evidence that confirms their hypothesis, and ignore or underweigh evidence that could disconfirm it.

Researchers have shown repeatedly that once people believe something strongly they are not likely to change their minds, even when presented with new factual information that proves their initial belief wrong. A study published in November 2015 ("The Power of Priors: How Confirmation Bias Impacts Market Prices") examined confirmation bias amongst financial analyst students. Professors Michael Cipriano and Thomas S. Gruca found that when student traders invested money in new movies based on their predicted four-week opening box office sales, the analysts continue to support their investments even when anticipated ticket sales fell far below what was predicted. In other words, even when the movie was not making money, the analysts continued to invest in stocks for the movie because they had previously predicted that it would make a good profit.

We have found that discussing how adult brains make errors helps students attend to information better as they proceed through the inquiry process. We expect that examples featuring adults helps students feel less defensive; they don't feel we are accusing them of making silly errors.

CONVICTION
Do you think you have any "pet theories" about teaching and learning that bias you against new approaches and possibilities?

COMMITMENT
During an inquiry, would you reflect upon your own confirmation biases and share them with your students? Why or why not?

Beliefs	Evidence	Impact of evidence
Financial students were asked to forecast what they believed would be the first month revenue of a new movie.	After the first month, actual revenue for the movie was significantly less than their forecast.	Students stuck to their intial forecast for the second month, in spite of actual sales and the prospect of financial loss.

FIGURE 5.6 No one is immune from confirmation bias. It is a powerful phenomenon that can lead to serious errors of thinking, decision-making and judgment.

Memory bias

A third brain error that can impact the synthesis process is memory bias. A memory bias either enhances or impairs the recall of a memory or alters the content of a reported memory. Different types of memory bias are described in Figure 5.7.

In general, we want students to be aware of the fact that it is normal for our brains to make errors when processing information. It is important that they, and we, are aware of cognitive biases and try to mitigate their impact while synthesizing information.

Type of bias	Technical description	For the junior learner
Self-generation bias	Self-generated information is remembered best. For instance, people are better able to remember statements that they have made than similar statements made by others.	You are more likely to remember what you did or said yourself than what someone tells you.
Illusion-of-truth effect	People are more likely to believe statements to be true when they have heard the statement before (even if they cannot consciously remember having heard them), regardless of the actual validity of the statement. In other words, a person is more likely to believe a familiar statement than an unfamiliar one.	The more times something is told to you, the more likely you are to believe it is true (whether it is true or not).
Misinformation effect	Remembered thoughts become less accurate because of interference from post-event information. That is, a discussion that occurs after an event can interfere with the accurate recall of the original information.	Discussing a memory may affect your ability to remember it accurately.
Illusory correlation	Inaccurately remembering a relationship between two events when there is none. In other words, a person may believe two events are related when they are not.	You may remember or believe that two events are related when they are not.

FIGURE 5.7 Do you think your students would be interested to learn the different ways their brains may fool them?

THINQ

• Which of these brain errors do you recognize in yourself and in your students?

• Would you attempt to run an activity or have a discussion with students about these brain errors before beginning the synthesis process? Why or why not?

5.3 How can I help students consolidate or "make sense" of evidence?

Every day we are bombarded with sensory stimulation. If our brains had to attend to every single piece of input, we would shut down. Have you ever noticed how you turn down the music in your car when you're driving in a new neighbourhood or city? You do this because you are concentrating very hard visually, so you need to reduce the auditory input you're receiving.

In this sense, children's brains work the same way as adults'. Children's brains naturally reject information that is too challenging or a task that appears too difficult. But teachers can help students overcome these synthesis challenges in a number of ways.

FOOD FOR THOUGHT

"People do not like to think. If one thinks, one must reach a conclusion. Conclusions are not always pleasant."

Helen Keller

Revisiting the inquiry question

Once students have finished the investigation phase of the inquiry — having gathered a variety of information, data or materials — they should return to their inquiry question. You can help them do this by distributing a consolidation template like the example in Reproducible 5A, *Student exploration: Making sense of my inquiry.* Regardless of the tool you use to help your students make sense of their evidence, the following key questions should help them with the consolidation process.

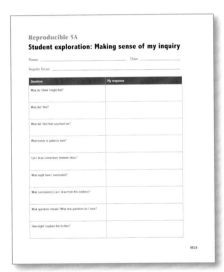

FIGURE 5.8 Reproducible 5A, p. RE28.

Questions to focus consolidation	
• What is my inquiry question? (What am I exploring?)	• Did I find anything surprising?
• What did I think I might find?	• What might I have overlooked?
• What did I find?	• Am I able to draw a conclusion?
• What patterns or trends exist in the evidence?	• What questions remain?
• Can I make connections between pieces of evidence?	• What additional questions do I now have?
	• What could I do to explore this further?

FIGURE 5.9 Pausing between evaluating evidence and drawing a conclusion can be an important step that avoids difficulties later on.

Identifying trends, patterns and connecting ideas

One way for students to consolidate or make sense of their evidence is to identify patterns or trends in the information they have collected. Patterns or trends are ideas, themes or arguments that repeat throughout the evidence. Students can be prompted to identify patterns and trends by considering questions such as the ones in Figure 5.10.

When making sense of evidence, students can also look for connections between ideas. These connections can be between their *own* ideas and the evidence, or connections between the ideas *expressed in the evidence* they have collected. For example, students make connections between their own ideas and the evidence when they respond to the questions "What did I wonder?" and "What did I find?" Students will also make connections when they find three similar ideas expressed in the evidence they have collected.

What is **similar** about the evidence?

Can you see any **patterns**?
What do they tell you?

Are there **consistent characteristics** across a number of pieces of evidence?

Can you see any **trends**?
What do they tell you?

What evidence **fits together** and why?
What is **not a good fit** and why?

FIGURE 5.10 Asking a few key questions can be very helpful when trying to make sense of a body of information, data and evidence.

5.4 What are some simple tools to help students draw conclusions?

At the most basic level, drawing a conclusion is really about weighing the evidence related to a question under investigation. Most inquiries will have a number of "branches" of exploration and associated evidence. After students have consolidated their evidence they will have to make a decision about the inquiry question under investigation.

Keeping our junior learners in mind, we believe that it is important to provide tools that are very clear and uncomplicated to help students draw a conclusion. One suggestion we make is to project or provide the following "slice" of a checklist like the one in Figure 5.11 to help students reflect on their own progress during the synthesis process (see Reproducible 5B, *Student self-check: Making sense*).

Self-check: The synthesis process	Yes	Mostly	A little	Not yet
I made thoughtful conclusions based on my research.				
I talked about my research and my conclusion with my peers.				
I wrote down useful feedback from my peers.				
I used the feedback I received to improve my conclusion.				

FIGURE 5.11 Synthesis is a thoughtful process that benefits from peer review and feedback.

BIG IDEA

Sound conclusions can be drawn only after a body of evidence is carefully weighed.

FOOD FOR THOUGHT

"We have the duty of formulating, of summarizing, and of communicating our conclusions, in intelligible form, in recognition of the right of other free minds to utilize them in making their own decisions."

Ronald Fisher

Reproducible 5B

Student self-check: Making sense

Name: ______________________ Date: ____________

Inquiry focus: ______________________________

Self-check: The synthesis process	Yes	Mostly	A little	Not yet
I made thoughtful conclusions based on my research.				
I talked about my research and my conclusions with my group or peers.				
I wrote down useful feedback from my group and peers.				
I used that feedback to improve my conclusion.				

Credit: Sonia Racco, York Region District School Board. Work completed as part of Inquiry-Based Learning Module, July 2015. Toronto, Ontario.

RE29

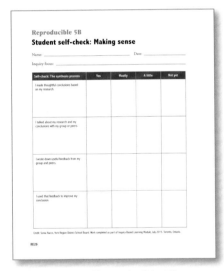

FIGURE 5.12 Reproducible 5B, p. RE29.

Many elementary school teachers also report that PMI charts help them with the inquiry process. The PMI (Plus, Minus, Interesting) chart was developed by Edward de Bono in 1982. De Bono was an early proponent of the deliberate teaching of thinking in schools. The PMI chart has many applications, but it was designed to be a quick tool (three to five minutes in length) to weigh the pros and cons of an issue, widen the perception of a problem or decision, or uncover issues that might have been overlooked.

In the context of inquiry we have found that many teachers use PMI charts (without a 5-minute length limit) to help students draw conclusions. A blank template is provided as Reproducible 5C, but a simple web search will provide you with a number of other formats to choose from.

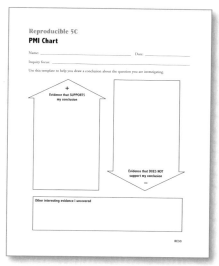

FIGURE 5.13 Reproducible 5C, p. RE30.

We have been working with teams of teachers to integrate more opportunities for inquiry into their lesson and unit plans. The lesson plan on the next page in Figure 5.14 contrasts traditional lesson plans for a grade 4 unit on light and sound with a more inquiry-based approach. The unit was was built around big ideas and outcomes from a local curriculum:

- Technological innovations involving light and sound have an impact on the environment.
- Light and sound are forms of energy with specific properties.

As you review the plan, consider how inquiry was integrated into each element of the plan in an explicit way.

THINQ

- How does the unit inquiry question compare to alternatives such as, "Do light and sound have an impact on humans?" or, "How are light and sound forms of energy?
- Specifically, what is one element of the revised unit that resonates with you?
- What further modifications might you make to this unit?

Lesson	Traditional unit	Inquiry-based unit
Inquiry question	• None	Do light and sound have an impact on the environment?
Opening	• Read from the textbook with accompanying worksheets identifying sources of light.	• Show a series of photos depicting various sources of light and sound. • Allow students to ask and discuss questions about what they see. • Use questions generated by students to guide the discussion about light and sound, and to inform subsequent lessons. (For example, student questions may point to a need to explicitly teach about properties of light and sound.)

Light	• Teach the definition of light energy explicitly.	• Have students use flashlights at two different times in the day to explore the properties of light.
		• Use prompts about properties of light to provide focus and help record evidence:
		  – "What is the difference between natural and artificial light?"
		  – "How are shadows made?"
		  – "How does light change/travel?"

Sound	• Play sound clips and ask students to identify what they hear.	• Play sound clips and ask students to identify what they hear.
		• Prompt students with the following questions:
		  – "What is the difference between sound and noise?"
		  – "Which sounds would you consider to be noise?"
		  – "What impact does noise have on humans and the environment?"
		  – "Is our classroom mostly full of sound or noise?"
		  – "How might sound or noise impact learning?"

Vibration	• Show a slide presentation on vibration and the physiology of the ear: how we hear sounds and sense vibrations.	• Use balloons, sound forks, glasses and other items that modify sounds. • Provide students with water and bowls to experiment with amplified sound and vibrations. • Have students record their data on an "Evidence Sheet." • Debrief with students on they found.
Consolidation	• Students complete a worksheet on elements of light and sound.	• Place students in pairs or groups of three and have them copy the inquiry question onto a sheet of paper. • Give students time to review all of the evidence they have collected over the series of lessons and develop a response to the question.
Assessment	• Students complete a short unit test.	• **Balanced assessment:** Observe and listen to student explorations to track evidence of inquiry thinking and learning. • **Pair/Share:** Connect pairs/groups of students and have them share their response to the inquiry question. Instruct each group to provide feedback on the other's answer. Give students time to incorporate this feedback. • **Debrief:** Have each group share the other group's answer with the class. This will improve attention and listening while sharing. • **Individual consolidation:** Have each student write or record their response to the inquiry question, providing evidence for their response. Ask each student to also state one additional question they have about light and sound.

FIGURE 5.14 This unit plan contrasts traditional lessons for a grade 4 unit on light and sound with a more inquiry-based approach.

Weighing the evidence and concluding

Not all of the evidence students consider will be equally important or useful. Students need to weigh the evidence if they are to sort and filter their data. Figure 5.15 offers some criteria to consider. Reproducible 5D, *Balance of evidence* asks students to "pile up" the evidence they have in support of the inquiry question under investigation. The side with more evidence is the side they would argue answers the inquiry question. Although we do not want students to see inquiry questions as either "right" or "wrong," for the junior learner it is likely best not to complicate the process of drawing a conclusion with too many layers, at least in the beginning. Our hope is that as junior learners gain sophistication with the consolidation process, they will start to consider evidence that is ambiguous and illustrates the grey areas of their inquiry question.

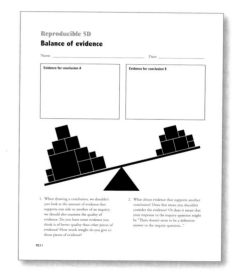

FIGURE 5.16 Reproducible 5D, p. RE31.

Is some evidence **more important** or useful in answering the inquiry question than other evidence?

Is there **more evidence** supporting one conclusion over others?

Does any of the evidence **conflict** or support totally different conclusions?

FIGURE 5.15 Because not not all of the evidence will be equally important or useful, it is important for junior learners to begin to weigh the value information relative to their objective.

Drawing conclusions in grade 5 science

Emma and Justin are grade 5 teachers and their students have been working on a science unit on energy sources. The inquiry question they provided to the class was "Should alternative energy sources replace the use of fossil fuels in our community?"

They provided their students with an evidence bundle containing photos, data tables, headlines, and short excerpts from reports. There were also various text books in the classroom.

Today, Emma and Justin distributed Reproducible 5D: *Balance of evidence* to their students and asked them to draw a conclusion about the inquiry question based on the evidence they had collected and considered. Emma and Justin met in the staff room at the end of the day to debrief.

Emma: I decided to do a Minds On in class today about balance of evidence by borrowing a scale from the science lab. I placed gram weights one at a time on opposite sides of the scale and talked about weight and balance, and how this also applies to evidence.

Justin: That's a great idea, I'll try that next time. I walked them through the Scales of Evidence handout, but your lesson launch was more engaging than mine. I was surprised by what I observed when they were attempting to draw conclusions today.

Emma: Why? What specifically surprised you?

Justin: Well, most kids simply listed the evidence they had on each side of the scale without giving any consideration to whether or not each piece of evidence was solid or not.

Emma: Right, I noticed that with my students too. I realized halfway through class that I need to talk about different types of evidence, and that drawing a conclusion is affected by more than just the amount of evidence they have. I actually think I may have lead them astray by using the physical scales at the beginning of class the way I did.

Justin: Well, I don't know about that. I didn't use the scales and our students seemed to proceed in a similar fashion. Although, I did observe that a few students gave some pieces of evidence greater weight than others. For example, one group drew a large box around one piece of evidence to indicate that it was significant.

Emma: Right, and I was blown away when one pair of students was talking about the fact that if they had more evidence they might come to a different conclusion.

Justin: Wow, that is amazing. Well I think that before I do this lesson again I would definitely raise some of these points about the weight of evidence with the class before I let them begin.

Emma: Yes, we will have to put our heads to come up with some engaging examples to explain these points.

THINQ

- What points in Emma and Justin's discussion resonated with you?

- How long do you think this debrief would have taken? Are you able to find time to debrief with your colleagues on a regular basis?

- Would it be beneficial if your principal reserved time for small grade team debriefing sessions into monthly staff meetings?

5.5 How do I assess the consolidation phase of the inquiry process?

In Chapter 2, *Assessing and evaluating* we suggested that the six essential abilities of inquiry learners are at the core of inquiry activities and inquiry assessment. The abilities to make sense, synthesize and consolidate are crucial at every stage of an inquiry. For example, a student cannot formulate a response to an inquiry question without "asking questions" about the evidence they have collected and they cannot conclude an inquiry without consolidating or "putting it all together." Reproducible 5E, *Assessment planning template: Puts it all together* can be used to plan your triangulated assessment evidence collection. Reproducible 5F, *Inquiry rubric and self-check: Puts it all together* can be used as an assessment *for* and *as* learning tool.

THINQ

- How do you currently assess the synthesis phase of the inquiry process?

- Is this an area in which you feel proficient, or do you feel you would benefit from further professional learning on this aspect of inquiry?

- Where might you be able to inject more assessment for learning into class time devoted to synthesis? What would be the benefits of doing so?

FIGURE 5.17 Reproducible 5E, p. RE32.

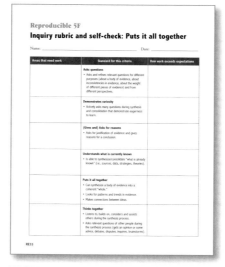

FIGURE 5.18 Reproducible 5F, p. RE33.

BIG IDEA

The ability to "put it all together" is an essential ability of the inquiry learner.

INQUIRY FOR ALL

Proficiency takes time and practice

It is worth remembering that like all important skills, consolidation and synthesis skills take time to develop. Providing plenty of class time to complete tasks can increase success. Thinking takes time, and we need to provide it. For many of us, this will require pushing back against overly packed classroom schedules that demand a certain number of minutes for each subject in a cycle.

You can also model these skills for students before asking them to try it. This doesn't have to take a huge amount of preparation. A simple Think Aloud where you try to solve a riddle or put the pieces of a puzzle together to reveal the "whole" can be enough to illustrate what consolidation looks and sounds like. After that, walking students through whatever consolidation tool you are asking them to use (such as a PMI Chart or Balance of Evidence graphic) will be a big help.

Revisit and reflect

This chapter looked closely at how teachers can best help students "make sense" of all the evidence they collect or are given during an inquiry. We shared our belief that it is worth taking the time to help students understand that conducting the deep thinking required by the synthesis process is hard, and that our brains can actually make mistakes when processing information.

We explored a number of ways that teachers can assist students with the synthesis process, including:

- having students explicitly revisit the inquiry question under investigation,

- working deliberately with concept maps,

- identifying patterns and trends in evidence and making connections between ideas, and

- providing simple tools to help students draw conclusions.

We considered a traditional and inquiry-based example of a science unit on light and sound as a way to reflect on how teachers could inject an inquiry approach into their current teaching and assessment materials. We concluded by reviewing a number of assessment tools specifically developed to measure students' abilities to synthesize and consolidate evidence.

To conclude your exploration of this chapter, take some time to complete Reproducible 5G, *Teacher checklist: Synthesis and consolidation in my classroom.*

THINQ

- How might you be able to collaborate with other teachers to increase your confidence and expertise at facilitating this step of the inquiry process?

- How can you design collaboration opportunities for your students during the synthesis stage of inquiry?

- Which of the following big ideas from this chapter do you feel are the most important enduring understanding for you? What about for your students?

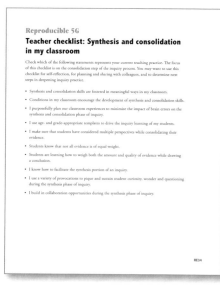

BIG IDEAS

5.1 When we synthesize a body of information we gain new knowledge.

5.2 The human brain often makes errors when processing information.

5.3 Synthesis or "making sense" is a complex process that requires teacher modelling and support.

5.4 Sound conclusions can be drawn only after a body of evidence is carefully weighed.

5.5 The ability to "put it all together" is an essential ability of the inquiry learner.

FIGURE 5.19 Reproducible 5G, p. RE34.

Chapter 6

REFLECTING AND SHARING:
Pushing learning to a deeper level

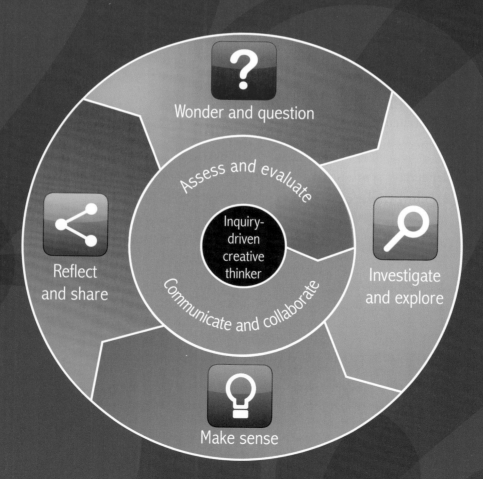

6.1 Why does reflection and sharing matter?

Since writing our previous book, *IQ: A Practical Guide to Inquiry-based Learning* (2014), we have spent hundreds of hours helping teachers plan inquiries, observing inquiry-based classrooms in practice, and reflecting with teachers about their experiences. We have seen that even in classrooms where teachers plan carefully and work hard to integrate inquiry-based learning, deep student thinking and understanding is not necessarily the outcome.

As a result of these experiences, we suggest that reflection and sharing be the final, explicit element of an inquiry process cycle. The goal of reflection and sharing is to push thinking to a deeper level. In fact, this stage of the inquiry process might just as well be called "reflection and sharing and reflection…" to suggest that every time we reflect and share, it causes us to reflect again.

So why haven't we found more reflection and sharing in inquiry-based classrooms? It may be as simple as the fact that some teachers don't explicitly build this final stage into their inquiries. They may build it into their inquiry plans by having students reflect and share at key times during an inquiry; for example, after the questioning, investigating, or making sense "stages" of the inquiry process. This is good planning and it is absolutely key to a successful inquiry.

However, once students have synthesized their learning and constructed an evidence-based response to the inquiry question, it is often the case that sharing and reflection ends. We believe that teachers can push learning to a deeper level by having students reflect on their conclusions, share with others, and then reflect again. The reflection and sharing process we are advocating here is really the the same process involved in good assessment *for* and *as* learning practices; this is not a new type of pedagogy.

In each chapter of this book we have highlighted opportunities where students can reflect and share. In this chapter we want to push learning deeper by encouraging teachers to plan for rich reflection and sharing at the end of an inquiry cycle.

BIG IDEA
Deep learning and understanding results from reflection and discussion with others.

CONVICTION
How convinced are you that reflection and sharing can deepen learning?

CAPACITY
What are the main obstacles to incorporating more reflection and sharing into your classroom?

FOOD FOR THOUGHT

"Life can only be understood backwards; but it must be lived forwards."

Soren Kierkegaard

"We don't learn from experience, we learn by reflecting upon experience."

John Dewey

"Without reflection, we go blindly on our way, creating more unintended consequences, and failing to achieve anything useful."

Margaret J. Wheatley

"Education begins the [person], but reading, good company and reflection must finish [them]."

John Locke

6.2 What does effective reflection and sharing look and sound like?

To paraphrase John Dewey, we do not learn from inquiry experiences — we learn from reflecting on inquiry experiences. Reflection asks us to pause and attend deliberately to our thinking processes and our lived experiences. It is at these crucial mental "check-in" points that we "go over" and "re-live" our experience. During reflection we may contemplate other possible choices, ask further questions, and consider future courses of action based on the conclusions of our reflective process.

Effective reflection

Reflection can take many forms. Reflection can happen during an action ("Let's pause and think.") or after an action ("Let's think about what I did and why."). Reflection occurs throughout all stages of an inquiry process and again at the end of the process.

Reflection works well when it is modelled and practiced on a regular basis. Reflections can be written on an exit card, in a journal or on a simple graphic organizer. Oral reflections can be shared with a teacher, students or family members. Reflections are most effective when students can see the impact of the reflection in helping them to improve their skills and deepen their learning. Reflections should be motivating and build confidence in junior learners.

Check in with your learners and ask them what type of reflection they like the best and the reasons for their preferences. Sometimes, reflection is considered by junior learners as the "throwaway" part of an activity, an unpleasant necessity that seems to interrupt their learning.

> **BIG IDEA**
>
> Both students and teachers need concrete examples of what good reflection and sharing look and sound like.

> **CONFIRMATION**
>
> How have sharing and reflection with colleagues helped clarify your thinking and improve your professional practice?

REFLECTION DURING inquiry LOOKS like ...

- Teachers modeling reflection, especially when "reflecting" is new.
- Students reflecting 2–3 times a week, 2–3 minutes at a time.
- Students reflecting quietly on their own.
- Students discussing and recording their reflections with a peer.
- Students responding to reflective prompts.
- Students considering samples of their peers' reflections.
- Students looking back at previous reflections and articulating their growth.
- Students writing in an inquiry journal, on an exit card, or on social media.

FIGURE 6.1 Reflection doesn't just happen. Teachers need to carve out time and space if it is to become a regular part of their inquiry classroom.

Make reflection as seamless as possible in your inquiry activities, and use oral and social media formats to increase student interest. Some teachers we have met use motivational and/or mindfulness techniques such as "reflection" music and/or reflection images (e.g., of nature, abstract art, people thinking) in addition to reflection prompts to cue students to the fact that it is time of quiet, individual serious thought. Once students have had time for individual reflection (which may or may not include writing), there should be time for students to share one aspect or part of their reflection with a peer or the teacher.

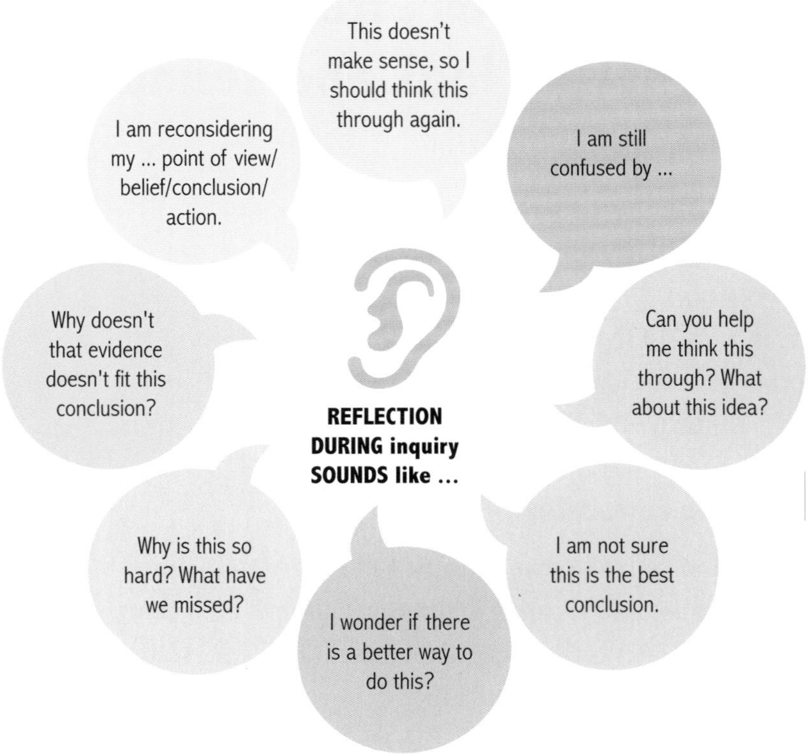

This doesn't make sense, so I should think this through again.

I am still confused by ...

Can you help me think this through? What about this idea?

I am reconsidering my ... point of view/belief/conclusion/action.

Why doesn't that evidence doesn't fit this conclusion?

REFLECTION DURING inquiry SOUNDS like ...

Why is this so hard? What have we missed?

I wonder if there is a better way to do this?

I am not sure this is the best conclusion.

FIGURE 6.2 As students reflect during their inquiry, you should hear expressions of confusion, rethinking, wondering, questioning and analysis.

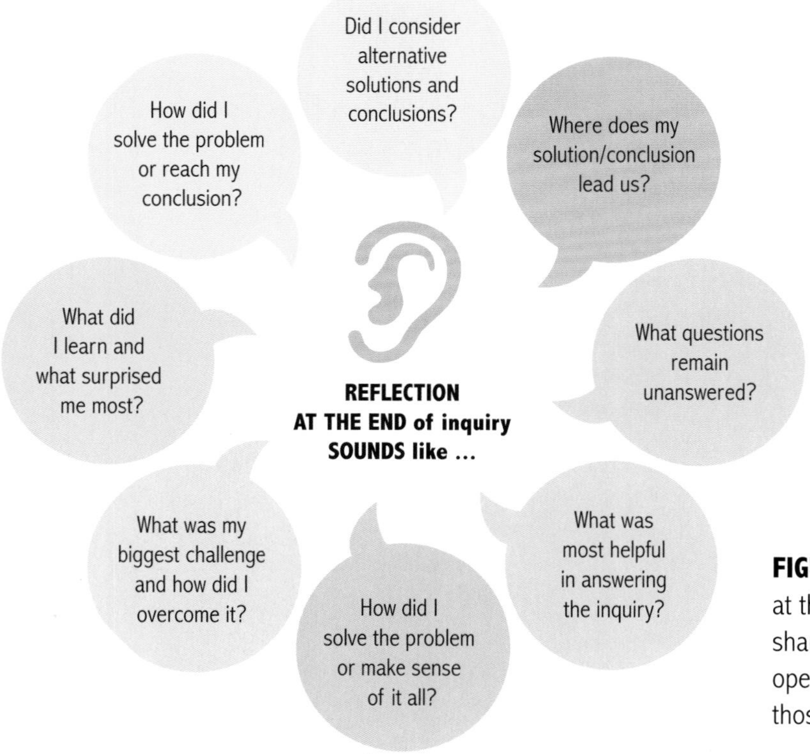

Did I consider alternative solutions and conclusions?

How did I solve the problem or reach my conclusion?

Where does my solution/conclusion lead us?

What did I learn and what surprised me most?

REFLECTION AT THE END of inquiry SOUNDS like ...

What questions remain unanswered?

What was my biggest challenge and how did I overcome it?

How did I solve the problem or make sense of it all?

What was most helpful in answering the inquiry?

FIGURE 6.3 For the junior learner, reflection at the end of the inquiry may be as simple as sharing the answers to these questions, being open to suggestions from others and acting on those suggestions.

Sharing at the end of an inquiry

Sharing the outcomes of an inquiry should be an exciting and celebratory time for junior learners. This is the time to highlight their unique thinking, solutions and creations. It should also be a time of support because inquiry demands a "double check" of thinking, solutions and creations by peers. Student work is not just "presented" as a static finished work; it becomes an invitation for others to participate and engage in the same question or problem.

My conclusion, based on the evidence I have considered so far, is …

My thinking up to this point is …

FIGURE 6.4 When conclusions are shared, they should be presented as a learner's thinking "up to this point" and as an invitation for others to engage. This highlights the fact that learning is an ongoing process and that conclusions change and evolve as we learn more.

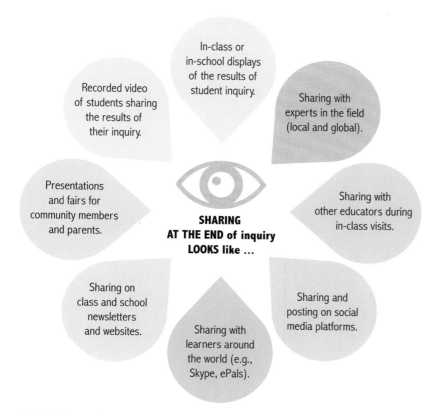

In-class or in-school displays of the results of student inquiry.

Recorded video of students sharing the results of their inquiry.

Sharing with experts in the field (local and global).

Presentations and fairs for community members and parents.

SHARING AT THE END of inquiry LOOKS like …

Sharing with other educators during in-class visits.

Sharing on class and school newsletters and websites.

Sharing with learners around the world (e.g., Skype, ePals).

Sharing and posting on social media platforms.

FIGURE 6.5 Sharing works best when teachers and schools create places, venues, connections and events specifically designed to help students share their inquiry work.

TECH-ENABLED INQUIRY

Sharing through technology

Junior students can get very excited when they share their inquiry journey with a wider audience. Social media apps make it easy for students to connect with other students at various stages of an inquiry. There are countless and free knowledge-sharing apps for students that can connect them to people with the same interests or to specific online communities. Some of these apps are website-building tools with simple and attractive interfaces. Other apps include large databases of general or themed information that is compiled, maintained and shared by an online user community. Many knowledge-sharing apps combine media clips, links and conversations that encourage others to participate in the discussion. Video sharing is another popular way to spread new knowledge resulting from inquiry learning.

Some of the common terminology used for this endpoint of an inquiry method is "sharing findings," "taking action," "improving" and "checking and extending." What each of these terminologies share is the idea that the conclusions of the inquiry are open for consideration and can be further deepened through collaboration with other students as " learner-experts." These learner-experts help to ensure the quality of the product. Students are learner-experts when they understand and can apply the criteria of an effective inquiry. Students that have participated in the co-creation of criteria for an effective inquiry and have had multiple opportunities to self-assess and peer-assess are skilled learner-experts.

The sharing stage of an inquiry is an opportunity to highlight inquiry dispositions for your students. Students should be encouraged to demonstrate curiosity, wonder and open-mindedness towards the learning of their peers. They can once again question, critique and provide new perspectives. An important aim in the sharing stage is for students to be "amazed" at the new learning discovered by their peers and to learn more about themselves as learners while witnessing the learning of others.

CONTEXT
Can you imagine your inquiry classroom full of the sights and sounds of reflection and sharing?

FIGURE 6.6 At the end of inquiry you can use these questions and comments to model, facilitate and gauge the nature of student sharing.

THINQ

• How might your students benefit from more frequent opportunities for sharing and reflection in your classroom?

• Do you anticipate obstacles or barriers to building reflection and sharing into your classroom routines?

• Which of the strategies listed above might prove to be the most successful for your students?

6.3 How do I get students to give and respond to supportive critique?

Our junior learners become (age-appropriate) experts in inquiry learning through experience, reflection and sharing. The endpoint of an inquiry cycle includes an important opportunity for collaborative, supportive and appreciative "critique." We have chosen to use the word *critique* instead of *feedback* to distinguish this as a specific stage of inquiry, as opposed to the more generic and ongoing feedback that is provided throughout all learning experiences, including inquiries.

"Sharing" our inquiry work with others is not a one-way experience. Inquiry sharing involves the student "presenting" their work and their peers "responding" back in a meaningful way. The presenting student is then called on to consider the critique and to improve their work.

This quality assurance process is found in many disciplines and professions. Chefs ask other chefs to test their food. Athletes have coaches or former athletes offer advice on their skills. Artists have contests and exhibits judged by peers. Writers engage in supportive critique sessions with other writers where they "meet and critique." Scientists, mathematicians and other professions have their work peer reviewed or refereed before it becomes published. You may want to share these professional examples with junior learners and ask them why supportive critique is important to learning.

> **BIG IDEA**
> Rich learning happens in response to reflecting on meaningful feedback and applying it to the work at hand.

> **CONTEXT**
> How do your junior learners give and respond to critique and feedback?

> **CONVICTION**
> Do you believe that junior learners have the capacity to get better at giving and receiving feedback?

FIGURE 6.7 Most junior learners will need to see and practise how to effectively give and receive a critique.

Offering a critique	Receiving and responding to a critique
• Use anchor charts, rubrics and exemplars that detail the quality of work expected. • Be positive and enthusiastic; tell the person what is effective and what is interesting. • Ask for clarification if you are unsure. • Raise a concern, but be clear and specific. • Don't give too many suggestions (focus on what is most important to improving the work). • Don't change the person's work on their behalf (e.g., spelling, rewriting, corrections).	• Listen carefully. • Don't be defensive or get angry. • Respond to suggestions by explaining further. • Ask questions if you don't understand the suggestion. • Say thank you. • Take action on suggestions that you feel will most improve your work. • Be prepared to explain why you rejected suggestions (if you do).

6.4 What are some practical tools to help students reflect and share?

We feel it is important to stress how worthwhile it is to regularly build in reflection and sharing sessions into your classroom routine. Teachers we have worked with tell us they were pleased and surprised by how much their students look forward to these sessions. They appreciate that their students enter the classroom asking, "Are we going to be reflecting and sharing today?" rather than asking, "Are we going to be doing anything interesting today?"

When reflecting and sharing become the norm in your classroom, you'll have created a community of learners. Students will have come to understand that thinking and knowing can be improved by sharing with others and receiving critiques of their work. They will also now appreciate that learning is an ongoing process, which is a very different classroom model than one that is anchored in the presentation of material from the teacher or the textbook followed by the reporting back of the "right" answer by the students.

We have taken many of the suggestions made in this chapter and created a few reproducibles that may help you incorporate more student sharing, critique and reflection into your classroom practice. Of course, these templates can also be used by students as guides to create digital reflections or to have conversations with other students or yourself; they do not have to be completed with pen or pencil. You may also choose to modify these templates to better meet the needs of your students.

FIGURE 6.8 Reproducible 6A, p. RE35. **FIGURE 6.9** Reproducible 6B, p. RE36.

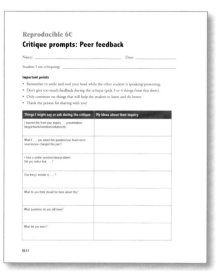

FIGURE 6.10 Reproducible 6C, p. RE37.

Observing students conduct a peer critique

Do I always have to use a BLM template?

Tarra and her grade team partners wanted to improve their students' reflection skills. Up to this point, their grade 5 students were enthusiastic peer "editors," but weren't particularly effective at helping a partner to push their thinking further. The team decided to model an effective peer critique to the entire class, carefully pair up their students, provide a critique template (Reproducible 6C), and then observe their students during the critiquing process.

Tarra selected a student named Ahmed, who she knew was outgoing and capable of handling feedback and suggestions very well. She sat with Ahmed at the front of the class, projected Reproducible 6C, *Critique prompts: Peer feedback* onto the screen and conducted a critique of his inquiry. Ahmed came up with some humorous answers in response to Tarra's prompts which Tarra liked because it made the process seem less threatening and more collaborative. At the conclusion of the modelling exercise, Tarra drew her students' attention to a couple of points that Ahmed could have handled differently. Her hope was that this would stretch her students' thinking further and make the point that there wasn't just one way to conduct a peer critique — there wasn't a "perfect" way to do it.

Tarra then asked the pairs to begin their own critiques. She circulated around the room making anecdotal notes of their progress, stopping to answer questions or redirect students as needed.

We want to acknowledge that it is often problematic working with a template someone else has provided because it may not suit the needs and/or language level of your own students. Another limitation of templates is that they tend to be linear. However, BLMs can often be a good way to get started, particularly the first time you conduct an inquiry.

We often simply cover student desks with large sheets of butcher paper and have students write their inquiry question at the top or in the middle of the sheet. Software such as SMART Ideas or Mindomo can also help students synthesize evidence.

THINQ

- How could you make or find the time to model the activities or tasks you want your students to perform? How might modelling or role-playing help your students?

- Are your students capable of conducting this peer critique exercise effectively? Do you think this exercise would improve the quality of their work? What skills might they gain?

Revisit and reflect

This chapter made the argument that it is important to build in frequent opportunities for sharing, critique and reflection throughout the inquiry process, including the final stage of the inquiry process.

You were asked to consider the benefits of sharing, critique and reflection for student learning. We explored what sharing and reflection look and sound like in the classroom, and we provided some practical strategies to help students become better at critiquing other's work and reflecting on their own learning.

In the next chapter, we examine the big ideas of inquiry that underpin a successful inquiry-based learning program and provide a planning model that has helped many teachers to integrate more inquiry into their teaching and assessment practice.

THINQ

- How might sharing, critique and reflection help push your students' learning and thinking to a deeper level?

- What is missed if teachers do not find the time to build sharing and reflection opportunities into each stage of the inquiry process, including the final stage of the process?

BIG IDEAS

6.1 Deep learning and understanding results from reflection and discussion with others.

6.2 Both students and teachers need concrete examples of what good reflection and sharing look and sound like.

6.3 Rich learning happens in response to reflecting on meaningful feedback and applying it to the work at hand.

6.4 Reflecting and sharing should be a regular occurrence in any inquiry classroom.

Chapter 7
WRAPPING IT UP:
What matters most

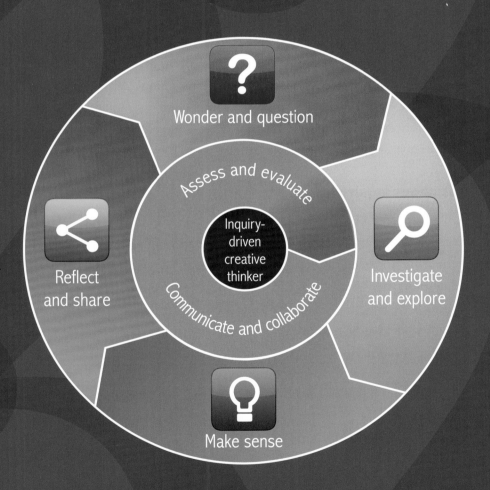

7.1 What are the big ideas of inquiry?

THINQ 4–6: Inquiry-based learning in the junior classroom has been written specifically for whom we refer to as junior learners — students in grades 4 to 6. We have argued that inquiry-based learning can capitalize on the curiosity and passion for learning that naturally resides in young learners.

Inquiry-based learning has a long theoretical history in education, but it has not been implemented in a systematic, integrated way in most schools and school boards. We believe it is possible to do so. We believe this book can help.

THINQ 4–6 identifies the big ideas that underpin a successful inquiry-based learning program and provides practical strategies for planning, instruction and assessment within this framework. To conclude this book, we summarize the twenty biggest ideas at the core of inquiry-based learning and present a ten-step model to plan for and do more inquiry.

Twenty big ideas about inquiry-based learning

In this section you'll find twenty big ideas that we feel are at the heart of inquiry-based learning. These ideas were explored throughout *THINQ 4–6* and represent the enduring understandings of this resource and pedagogy. You'll notice that they aren't organized around the stages of the inquiry process. This isn't because we believe that inquiry process models aren't useful, but rather that big ideas apply regardless of inquiry stage, discipline, grade level or educational environment. You may want to use these big ideas with your teaching partners, staff or senior administrators to plan for more inquiry in teaching and assessment programs.

1 We learn by asking questions (inquiring).

Inquiry learning is rooted in our innate desire to make sense of the mysterious world. When we ask questions, determine a problem, and use our heads and hearts to investigate what fascinates us, we are engaged in inquiry.

2 Inquiry dispositions support risk-taking and a sustainable commitment to inquiry learning.

Curiosity, open-mindedness and confidence in your ability to reason are inquiry dispositions — or what some call "inquiry habits of mind." They are what keeps the learner on the journey of inquiry. These dispositions support risk-taking and commitment to inquiry learning. They make us perseverant and accepting of failure and mistakes as an important part of the journey.

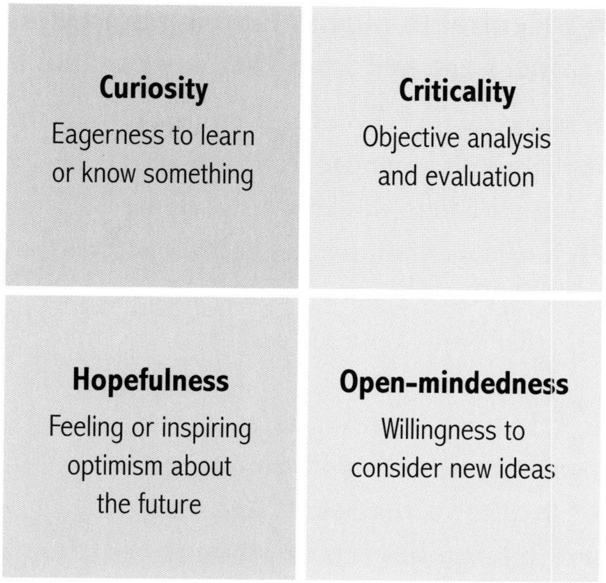

3 All knowledge is living and changing because it is personally and socially constructed.

Students learn best when they are invited to be part of the active and exciting process of knowledge building. Learners are no longer viewed as containers to be filled with disconnected bits of knowledge; they are naturally curious, rational and committed to making sense of their world. Teachers also teach best when they are intellectually engaged in their craft and not merely following lock-step curricular or instructional mandates.

4 All inquiry learning, regardless of grade or discipline, has three common essential traits.

All inquiry learning experiences share three traits: an essential question that invites the learner to wonder, think deeply and solve; answering the question or solving the problem using a method or process; and thinking critically, self-reflecting, contributing, communicating and sharing findings so that new knowledge is created.

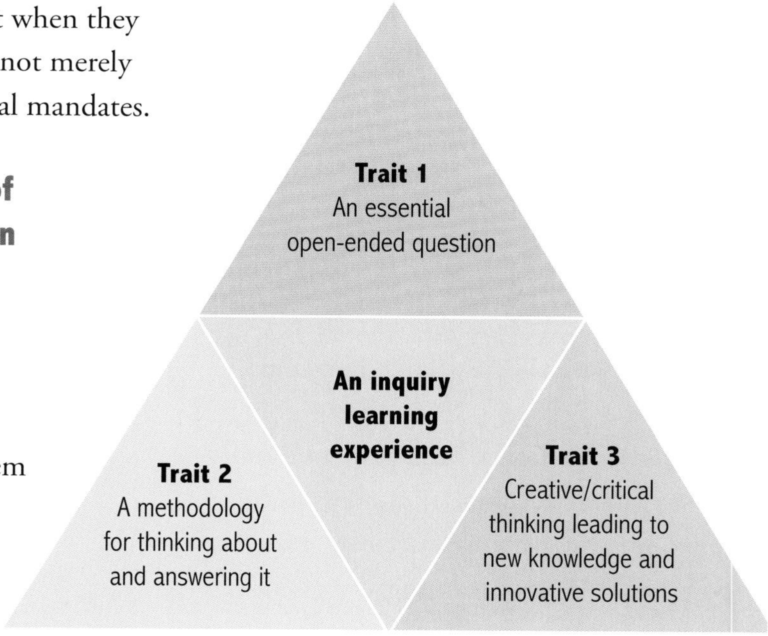

Curiosity
Eagerness to learn or know something

Criticality
Objective analysis and evaluation

Hopefulness
Feeling or inspiring optimism about the future

Open-mindedness
Willingness to consider new ideas

FIGURE 7.1 Inquiry dispositions

Trait 1
An essential open-ended question

An inquiry learning experience

Trait 2
A methodology for thinking about and answering it

Trait 3
Creative/critical thinking leading to new knowledge and innovative solutions

FIGURE 7.2 Essential traits of inquiry learning

5 **Central to inquiry learning are beliefs about who learners are and what they are capable of.**

Inquiry learning encourages human curiosity. It demands rational thought. It is grounded in what is already known but pushes the learner to add to this knowledge through a process in which they explore ideas from new perspectives and viewpoints. Learners are in control. They are active participants, not passive recipients. Learning is a collaborative endeavour.

6 **Inquiry learning is a continuum, with a large degree of teacher direction at one end and a large degree of student autonomy at the other.**

Open-inquiry is the long term goal. Teacher-directed and blended inquiry are practical classroom realities. A teacher's decision about the balance between teacher direction and student autonomy in an inquiry will depend on their assessment of the conditions in their classroom and the capacity and experience of their students.

FIGURE 7.3 Moving from guided to open inquiry

7 **At the heart of assessment are teachers and students asking, "How are we doing?"**

Assessment, in a fundamental way, is about teachers and students pausing to reflect independently on the question, "How am I doing?" and collectively, "How are we doing?" These questions relate to both academic and social-emotional learning. They allow us to consider our aims as individual learners and to empower and improve learning. Six essential abilities are at the core of inquiry activities and assessment.

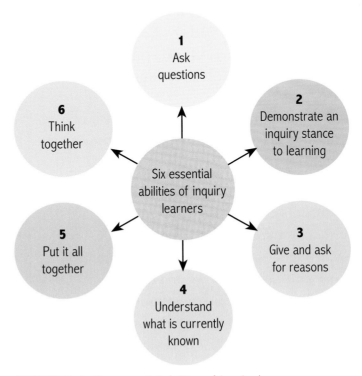

FIGURE 7.4 The essential abilities of inquiry learners

8 Curriculum should be seen not as the end, but as the means to engage students in rich learning activities.

Curriculum should be regarded as a means, not an end. If our aim is for students to engage in rich, personally and socially significant learning activities that target big ideas and enduring understandings, then the items that make up curriculum become the means and context to carry out this learning. However, a desire to cover every aspect of the curriculum will likely restrict your ability to plan and implement inquiry-based learning.

9 Students should be our assessment partners.

Students should have a say in what to aim for, what quality looks like, and how to demonstrate their learning. Authentic snapshots of learning are not just possible, but practical with new handheld technologies that allow students to capture their thinking to share with peers, teachers and parents. Inquiry assessment is an iterative three-stage process that involves gathering, interpreting and responding to evidence of a student's inquiry skills and dispositions.

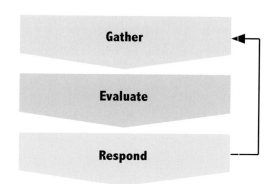

FIGURE 7.5 The inquiry assessment process

10 Our curiosity fuels our learning.

Inquiry begins with wondering. Learning begins with questions. We are all curious about the way the world works. Our curiosity fuels and gives purpose to our learning. We can sense when wonder is at work in our students — they are fascinated and focused. Questions arise. Creativity and critical thinking abound. At these moments, the learner feels excited and determined to dive deeper into their learning.

11 The purpose of an inquiry question is to entice your students to think deeply about the mysteries of life.

Inquiry questions are helpful to learners because they stimulate thinking and feeling, and they drive learning by signalling what is truly essential and fascinating about their world. They can often be deceptively simple, but they cannot be simply answered.

12 **Questions that elicit strong emotions are often the best place to begin.**

Often teachers and students aren't sure about whether their questions are "good" questions. One key criterion of a good inquiry question is whether it evokes strong emotions and feelings. If the question generates debate and controversy, you've likely got yourself a good question.

13 **We need to describe exactly what good thinking involves and encourage students to be attentive to their own thinking.**

Inquiry-based learning requires considerable amounts of reasoning, which may pose challenges for many junior students. We can't just ask students to "think harder" — we need to describe exactly what good thinking involves and encourage students to be attentive to their own thinking, even when we are not there prompting them to do so.

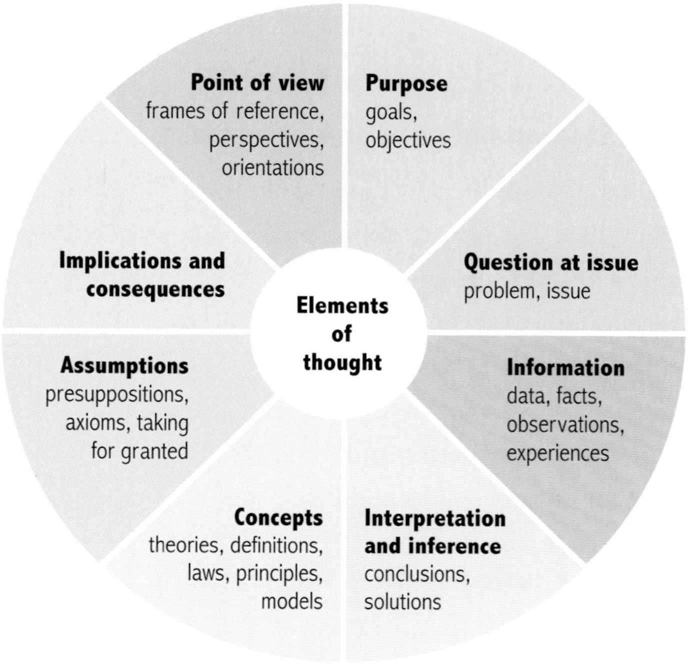

14 **Teachers need to help students become better questioners.**

Questioning is a crucial inquiry skill and is found in each method of inquiry and at each stage of every model. Students need to be explicitly taught how to develop good questions and become good questioners. This requires the development and application of criteria.

FIGURE 7.6 The eight elements of thought

15 **Constructing a rich response to a question is more appealing when students know there is no predetermined "correct" answer.**

Too often, our expectation is that students should "get the right answer." However, this doesn't often require deep thinking, since students rarely encounter anything that is debatable or inconclusive. Yet what is debatable is often the most interesting and stimulating. We need to engage students by asking them to investigate questions that have many valid and sometimes contradictory answers.

16 Teachers need to be both leaders of and co-learners alongside their students.

It is good for students to see that their teachers don't have all the answers. No one does! If the answers are already known, what learning really takes place when answering those questions? Rote learning and memorization are very different from deep thinking. As students develop their inquiry skills, and teachers gain more experience facilitating inquiry-based learning, the role of the teacher will naturally evolve to meet the unique needs of students from year to year.

17 Teachers need to model an inquiry stance as well as provide parameters and structures to ensure student success.

Teachers should support students during the inquiry process by planning to uncover preconceived ideas and misconceptions, locating a selection of age- and grade-appropriate sources from a variety of perspectives, and helping students assess the credibility of sources.

18 When we synthesize a body of information we gain new knowledge.

The creation of new knowledge often, but not exclusively, comes after a body of evidence is synthesized or consolidated. Synthesis, or what we call "making sense" for junior learners, like other elements of thinking and learning, needs to be taught explicitly.

19 Sound conclusions can be drawn only after a body of evidence is carefully weighed.

At the most basic level, drawing a conclusion is really about weighing the evidence. Most inquiries will have a number of "branches" of exploration and associated evidence. Only after students have consolidated their evidence can they begin to effectively draw conclusions or develop solutions.

20 Deep learning and understanding results from reflection and discussion with others.

Teachers can push learning to a deeper level by having students reflect on their conclusions, share with others, and then reflect again. The reflection and sharing process in an inquiry is really the same as best practice assessment *for* and *as* learning, so this is not a new type of pedagogy.

CAPACITY
Which of these big ideas are already part of your teaching and assessment practices?

COMMITMENT
Which of these big ideas would you like to incorporate into your practice moving forward?

7.2 How do I move forward from here?

Many new curriculum guidelines and school board directives are embracing inquiry-based learning as a key objective. We believe this is because inquiry-based learning is a bridge to successful teaching and learning in the digital age. It will be well worth the investment to build your capacity to work within an inquiry-based learning framework.

In the end, the only way to learn to do inquiry is to do inquiry. We suggest you plan your early inquiries with the big ideas in mind. If you plan according to the big ideas of inquiry, then rich learning will happen regardless of whether or not the inquiry itself "goes" the way you originally imagined. There are a number of ways to plan an inquiry. We have sketched out one approach that has proven successful for many teachers.

1 Start with a guided inquiry.

We suggest you begin with a guided inquiry. There is lots of time for your students to conduct their own student-driven inquiries *after* they have experience and expertise with inquiry-based learning. We believe that starting with guided-inquiry is the best way to create the conditions that lead to student success.

2 Determine your broad curricular targets.

All inquiries are about something and it's up to you to decide which area of the curriculum you want to target. Make sure you are working from broad curricular targets (sometimes called "overall expectations" or "overarching targets" in curricula) rather than the list of small specific expectations that so often fill curriculum guidelines. Working from broad curriculum targets will give students choice within the inquiry experience you design. You can choose from different curriculum areas to build a great inquiry that bridges language arts, social studies and science, for example.

FOOD FOR THOUGHT

"For the things we have to learn before we can do them, we learn by doing them."
Aristotle

10 steps to doing more inquiry

1. Start with a guided inquiry.
2. Determine your broad curricular targets.
3. Develop rich inquiry questions from your targets.
4. Locate and collect grade- and age-appropriate sources to drive the inquiry.
5. Build in opportunities for ongoing sharing and reflection.
6. Create an assessment and evaluation plan.
7. Create and reinforce vocabulary to communicate inquiry thinking.
8. Help students make sense of the evidence.
9. Assist students in drawing conclusions based on their evidence.
10. Include time to reflect on and share conclusions.

FIGURE 7.7

③ Develop rich inquiry questions from your targets.

For inquiry-based learning to work effectively, students must start with an inquiry question that is both exciting and focused on the big ideas of a discipline. All effective inquiry questions have certain characteristics. You may choose to have the entire class work together on one inquiry question, or have groups of students investigate three or four questions looking at different aspects of the curriculum targets you have selected.

④ Locate and collect grade- and age-appropriate sources to drive the inquiry.

We want to stress that building a "starter" set of inquiry resources is well worth it. It will ensure that students consider resources with a variety of perspectives and increase the chances they will have an enjoyable and successful inquiry experience. Even better, since a rich question can lead to different evidence-based conclusions, you can use a source collection over many years. Sources can be dynamic too, as you add to and update your bundles based on classroom experience.

⑤ Build in opportunities for ongoing collaboration, sharing and reflection.

One of the fundamental qualities of inquiry is that students work together to make sense of a question or problem. Plan on having students work together at least some of the time. Providing regular opportunities for students to discuss and reflect on their learning, and to loop back to reconsider, revise, and/or restructure their thinking will help them understand more about not only the inquiry, but about themselves and their classmates as thinkers and learners.

An effective inquiry question...	
1 ... is an invitation to think (not recall, summarize or detail).	**2** ... comes from genuine curiosity and/or confusion about the world.
3 ... makes you think about something in a way you haven't before.	**4** ... invites both deep thinking and deep feelings.
5 ... leads to more good questions.	**6** ... asks you to think about the essential ideas in a discipline.

FIGURE 7.8 Qualities of effective inquiry questions

6 Create an assessment and evaluation plan.

Assessment bridges teaching and learning. It identifies where the learner is going (by establishing and sharing big ideas, concepts, fundamental skills, related learning goals and success criteria); where the learner is right now in their learning (by observing students, having conversations and assessing products); and how to get the learner to their goal (through the use of peer, self- and teacher feedback). Remember, students need to be partners in the assessment process, providing peer feedback and reflecting and reporting on their own learning. Students can be assessed through observation and conversation, not just the end product.

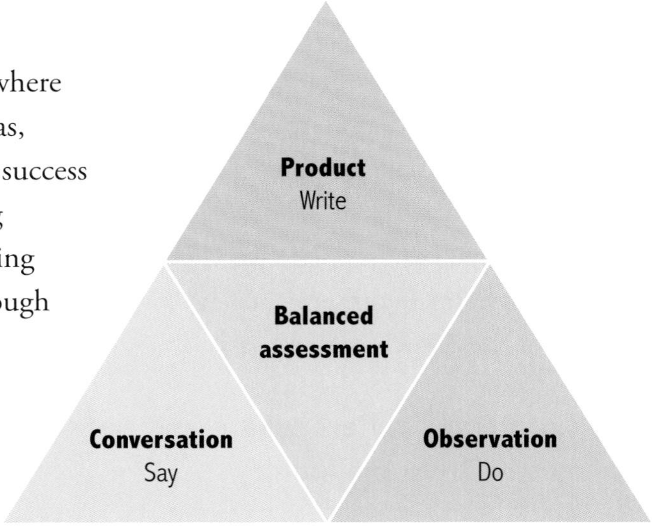

FIGURE 7.9 Elements of balanced assessment

7 Create and reinforce vocabulary to communicate inquiry thinking.

Communication is the way that students make their learning visible. Effective communication requires the integration of inquiry vocabulary into your daily classroom tasks. Over time, you should notice a new and powerful common language being spoken by your students. The strategies in Figure 7.10 will help you to develop such a vocabulary amongst your students.

8 Help students make sense of the evidence.

Whether you provide a full or partial bundle of sources for your students, or have students gather their own evidence, you will need to teach them how to make sense of their data. This includes helping them to consider the quality, reliability, usefulness and perspective of their sources.

Strategies for building inquiry vocabulary

- Create anchor charts or word walls of key inquiry vocabulary.

- Have students complete an inquiry journal where they articulate their understanding of new inquiry vocabulary as it arises.

- When listening to collaborative groups, ask questions that invite students to explain their understanding of key inquiry vocabulary in relation to the work they are completing.

- Students can create T-charts, Venn diagrams or other key visuals to define key inquiry vocabulary words or to compare two or more key inquiry vocabulary words.

- Have inquiry vocabulary "check-ins" by asking students comprehension and application questions. You can create the questions, or even better, have students create the questions on specific terms to assess their peers.

FIGURE 7.10

9 Assist students in drawing conclusions based on their evidence.

Help your students draw conclusions by having them identify patterns and trends, reflect on the quality of evidence, and consider whether the evidence supports one side of the inquiry question or the other (or a bit of both). Remember, a key goal is for students to understand that their conclusions should be based on their analysis of evidence. Others working from the same sources may come up with an entirely different evidence-based conclusion. This is to be encouraged, and it will be a sign that the inquiry question was rich and powerful.

10 Include time to reflect on and share conclusions.

It seems counter-intuitive to us that after a period of rich learning, students would keep their learning to themselves. We advocate that students share and reflect on their learning throughout the inquiry process. Students should also share and critique each other's work at the conclusion of the inquiry. This pushes learning to a deeper level. It promotes the idea that learning is an ongoing process and that new information and discussion could lead to a different conclusion.

THINQ BIG

Teamwork, sharing and building networks

There is a saying that "many hands make light work." This is a powerful idea when it comes to doing more inquiry. Designing questions and units, finding and creating inquiry resources, and reflecting on classroom experiences and student learning by yourself is a daunting prospect. Sharing with school colleagues and grade teams, building professional learning communities, and creating or joining online networks of like-minded educators is a necessary part of doing more inquiry.

The Internet and social media platforms offer unprecedented opportunities to share the results of your inquiry and to follow other educators. Share, post and blog the results of your efforts and seek out the work of others. Remember that many educators would love to learn about your inquiry experiences.

So whatever else you do, THINQ BIG! Connect yourself to teachers in your school, district and around the world. Think of yourself as a member of a team. Join an ever increasing number of educators working to change not only their own instructional practices, but the very nature of teaching and learning in a digital age.

BOOK STUDY NOTES

We were fortunate to have chapters of this book reviewed by gifted educators across the country. These advisers raised a number of thoughtful points about inquiry-based learning that we thought would be very useful to drive a book study about *THINQ 4–6: Inquiry-based learning in the junior classroom.* We hope you find these questions helpful.

1. George Couros talks about effective staff development as moving individual teachers from their own Point A to Point B, rather than moving all teachers to a prescribed line that has been determined by someone else. If you apply this idea to your own learning, what is your current Point A when it comes to inquiry-based learning, and what is your Point B?

2. In many regards, inquiry-based learning seems logical and intuitive: we know that children and adults become highly engaged and perform at their best when questions are at the heart of learning. If we know this to be true, why is inquiry-based teaching and learning not the norm within our schools?

3. Some education experts feel strongly that unless student-driven inquiry is at the core of the learning process, then "inquiry" is not really happening. In this text, Colyer and Watt argue that thoughtfully planned, teacher-guided inquiry is the best way to integrate more inquiry into classroom instruction and assessment because directed inquiry increases the chances that students will succeed during inquiry. Where do you stand on this issue? Is it possible for both of these positions to be correct?

4. One of the key points the authors make in this book is that educators shouldn't think about inquiry-based learning as an all-or-nothing proposition. Instead, the goal is for educators to integrate more inquiry-based instruction and assessment into the work they already do in classrooms. If this is the goal, identify three to five areas of your own practice where you could integrate some aspect of inquiry-based learning.

5. Although some educators have larger blocks of time available within their timetables to facilitate inquiry-based learning, many do not. As a result, educators across the country have been experimenting with ways to incorporate inquiry into small pockets of time, e.g., 30 minutes of class time. This has turned out to be a good way for some educators to make their first steps into inquiry-based learning. What are some ways that inquiry could be facilitated in your classroom or school in 30 minute blocks, 60 minute blocks, or half days?

6. Some people speculate we are already moving from the Knowledge Age to the "Age of Creativity," where people must be highly skilled in producing creative opportunities and innovative solutions. If inquiry-based learning is a critical teaching and learning tool and the means to the end — where fostering "inquiry-driven creative thinkers" is the "end" — how critical is inquiry-based learning to the future of public education?

REPRODUCIBLES

Student exploration: What is inquiry?

Name: _____ Date: _____

Inquiry is a method of thinking that helps us to ask and answer deep and complex questions and solve important problems.

1. Which of the following do you think is a deep question or problem? Explain why you think so.

   a. Should I go to my friend's house after school today?

   b. How can we make our school more eco-friendly?

   c. How can we make a better cell phone?

   d. What is $150 \div 5$?

   e. What is the capital of Canada?

   _____

   _____

2. State an example of a deep/complex question that interests you.

   _____

   _____

   _____

3. What makes some questions easier to answer than others?

   _____

   _____

4. What do you think you might have to do in order to answer a deep question or problem in an effective way?

   _____

   _____

Student exploration: Curiosity is key

Name: _____ Date: _____

Have you ever wondered how something got to be a certain way, or why people act the way they do, or how something works, or how you could make something better?

If so, you have one of the most important qualities of an inquiry learner — you are curious!

Think about yourself as an inquiry learner by answering the following questions:

1. What makes you curious?

   _____

   _____

2. What do you feel like when you are curious?

   _____

   _____

3. Do you think it's important to be curious about the world? Why?

   _____

   _____

4. In what ways do your parents, caregivers, teachers and friends encourage your curiosity?

   _____

   _____

5. Is it possible to be bored if you are a curious person? Why or why not?

   _____

   _____

Student exploration: I'm an inquiry learner!

Name: _____ Date: _____

An inquiry learner enjoys wondering about the world, asking and answering questions and solving problems.

- They like to discover, create, improve and innovate.
- They enjoy playing with ideas.
- They are open-minded to the ideas of others.
- They are not afraid of making mistakes.
- They don't give up on learning.
- They seek the ideas of others but don't accept everything they hear, see or read.
- They want to know more.

Thinking about the description of an inquiry learner above, complete the following statements:

1. I am an inquiry learner because...

   _____

   _____

2. My goal in becoming a better inquiry learner is...

   _____

   _____

3. My teacher and fellow students could help me become a better inquiry learner by...

   _____

   _____

The inquiry process

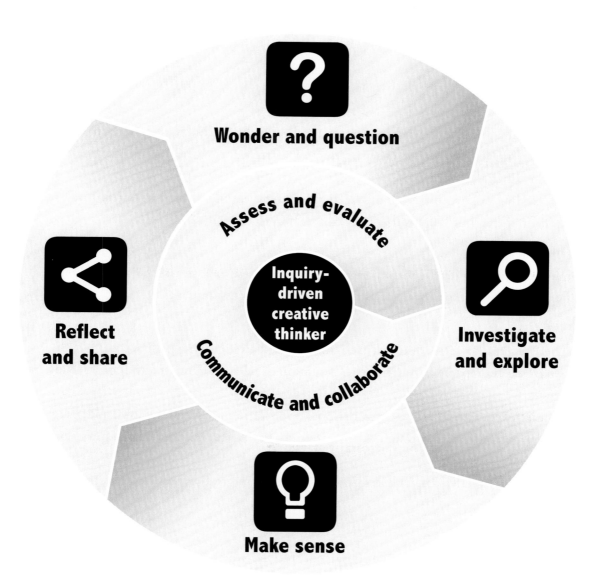

Teacher self-assessment: Which pattern of inquiry best describes your practice?

Which pattern(s) bests describes inquiry work in your classroom? Set preliminary goals on where you would like to proceed and how best to proceed to improve inquiry learning in your classroom.

Pseudo Inquiry

- A very traditional approach to teaching content and skills that includes a final inquiry-like project; often a written product or other product of research for which students have not been intentionally prepared.
- Discovery learning opportunities are provided for students. Students have opportunities to explore and/or create, but there is no direct connection to the skills of inquiry.

Emerging Inquiry

- Experimenting with inquiry by introducing inquiry exercises, such as asking questions for a specific purpose or assessing sources as in-class activities or assignments.

Guided Inquiry

- The teacher structures a series of units, each built around an inquiry experience, for which students have been prepared through the presentation of relevant content and inquiry skills development.
- A final inquiry experience that may include some opportunity for student choice and design. Students have been prepared through the presentation of relevant content and inquiry skills development.
- A series of inquiry experiences, each designed to address a targeted content area and to develop the skills of inquiry.

Inquiry

- An inquiry experience, perhaps student designed, through which students acquire content relevant to the inquiry and further develop their inquiry skills.

Adapted from the research of Virginia S. Lee, *What is Inquiry-Guided Learning?* (2012).

Teacher self-assessment: Inquiry readiness checklist

Check which of the following statements represents your knowledge, beliefs and understanding of inquiry learning. Use this checklist for self-reflection, for planning and sharing with colleagues, and to determine next steps in deepening your inquiry practice.

Conviction

- I believe in the main assumptions of inquiry-based learning: that learning is constructivist, student-centred and demands critical thinking.
- I am familiar with and convinced by the research that supports inquiry to improve student engagement and learning.

Commitment

- I am committed to bringing more inquiry-based learning to my classroom and have reflected on not only what makes me excited about inquiry learning, but also what makes me uncertain.
- I have connected with other committed educators who are interested and supportive of inquiry education.

Capacity

- I understand that inquiry is a process used to answer questions, solve problems and make new knowledge.
- I understand that a guided inquiry is a highly-structured and thoughtfully designed endeavour that allows for optimal student autonomy.
- I know there are distinct stages involved in an inquiry process.
- I understand that there are many inquiry models to choose from but that these models share essential traits.
- I understand that inquiries are on a continuum from guided to open (and that a degree of guidance is essential for effective student learning).

Context

- I understand what my role should be in an inquiry classroom.
- I accept that inquiry learning in my classroom should a be "playful," "messy," complex, recursive, iterative, non-linear experience and not merely a lock-step process to completing a product.
- I have thought about my students' readiness for inquiry and know where to start.

Confirmation

- I know what my professional goals are with respect to doing more inquiry.
- I understand how I will assess my progress, what is working and how to improve.

How to model and assess inquiry dispositions

Name: _____ Date: _____

Inquiry disposition	What it looks like in a classroom	How inquiry-based learning supports this disposition	Student reflection prompts
Curiosity and wonder	Teachers and students want to know more about the world and its people. They ask important, deep relevant questions. These questions are not answered easily - nor does the teacher or student have the correct answer in mind at the outset. They are honestly perplexed by an issue/question/problem and have the motivation to uncover a possible answer/solution.	Inquiry-based learning begins with a question, a curiosity or a wondering related to the discipline.	*An important question that I find interesting is . . .* *I think it is important to answer this question because . . .* *The question is hard to answer because . . .* *I feel I'm becoming a better questioner because . . .*
Criticality	Teacher and students enjoy the challenge of thinking deeply. Teacher and students trust that they can figure out difficult problems by using their reason and intelligence. Teacher and students are willing to try out different types of thinking (i.e., critical, creative, reflective) and different points of view.	Inquiry-based learning proceeds when learners trust that they can harness their own skills of reasoning when confronted with a challenging question. Inquiry-based learning allows students to develop discipline-specific thinking skills as they collect, critically assess and evaluate sources and then generate conclusions.	*Even though I may make mistakes, I believe I can succeed in this inquiry because . . .* *When confronted with a problem I cannot answer at first, I feel that . . .* *I have used critical thinking in this inquiry to . . .* *The thinking skill I have found most helpful in this inquiry is . . .*
Hopefulness	Teacher and students see the world as it is and like to think how it can be improved. They care about and have a sense of purpose and commitment in their inquiries.	Inquiry-based learning is future oriented and involves problem-solving. It encourages students to create and share new knowledge and to be change agents.	*I think solving this problem is important because . . .* *I think I can solve this problem because . . .* *I think my ideas could make a difference because . . .* *This is how I went about making new knowledge . . .*
Open-mindedness	Teacher and students are genuinely interested in other perspectives and attitudes. They realize that the question is never fully answered and that knowledge is always being constructed. They are open to continual learning.	Inquiry-based learning demands that evidence and information is gathered from multiple sources that represent diverse perspectives. Inquiry-based learning is an adventure. It is typically not a linear process, but one with twists and turns. These intellectual surprises allow students to experience what true experts in the discipline feel when attempting to solve a problem.	*Different sources and points of view are important to consider in this inquiry because . . .* *The one perspective I am having difficulty understanding or finding evidence to support is . . .*

SOURCE: Adapted from J. Walsh and B. Sattes, *Thinking Through Quality Questioning*, Corwin Press (2011).

The six essential inquiry abilities for assessment

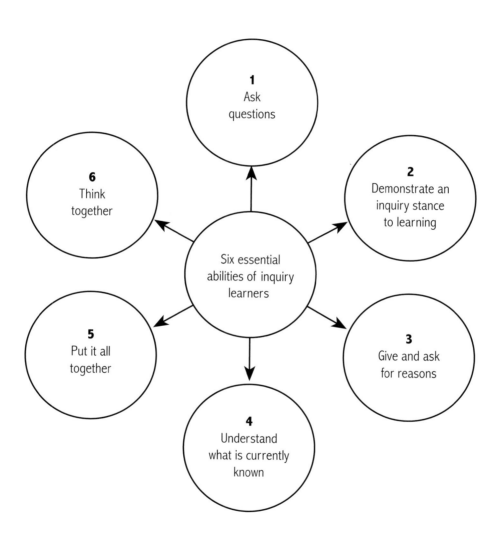

Student exploration: Who is an inquiry learner?

Name: _____ Date: _____

An inquiry is a way to go about solving an important problem or answering an important question. The following case study is an example of a problem that needs a solution.

Class 6B is having difficulty these days. There are two computers in the classroom and arguments result when more than two students want to use them for classwork.

Consider the comments made by students in Class 6B regarding this problem. Decide which of these students may be demonstrating the qualities of an inquiry learner and be prepared to explain your answer.

A. How are we supposed to figure this out — it's impossible! It's up to the teacher to fix the problem.

B. Let's do some math and figure out what might be a workable way to get computer time for everyone.

C. Can't we buy more computers instead of the new sports equipment?

D. We should ask the principal, our parents, and other teachers for their advice before we make a decision.

E. It's not a problem for me. I can do my work on my home computer.

F. Let's take the computers from the front office. Problem solved!

G. Let's create a point system. Whoever wins the most points gets the most computer time.

H. The school should allow us to bring our own devices. I wonder who may object to that and why, and who would support this idea and why.

I. Just because everyone likes using the computer doesn't mean they really need it. Let's talk about what is really essential to do on the computer versus what is convenient or fun to do. Then we could create a schedule based on need.

An inquiry rubric

Name: _____   Date: _____

Success criteria categories*	High degree of effectiveness	Considerable effectiveness	Some effectiveness	Limited effectiveness	Further support required
Inquiry skills and processes The student will: • ask and refine relevant questions that further the inquiry • investigate and explore sources that suggest answers and solutions • makes sense of the evidence and draw logical conclusions					
Application of thinking skills The student will: • use critical, creative and discipline-related thinking skills in order to provide an answer or course of action					
Communicate new understandings The student will: • communicate clearly and persuasively • engage the audience • use the vocabulary and terminology of the discipline					
Learn what is currently know about the question/problem The student will: • demonstrate knowledge and understanding of content important to the inquiry					

* Success criteria should be co-constructed between teacher and student as appropriate. Success criteria answer the question "What are the specific characteristics of a successful inquiry?"

Essential inquiry vocabulary

Inquiry action words	
Analyze	Examine something in detail
Assess	Consider the quality of something
Clarify	Make something easier to understand
Conclude	Decide something after thinking or research
Defend	Speak in favour or a person or idea
Explore	Look at something in a careful way to learn more about it
Evaluate	Judge something based on certain criteria
Investigate	Discover and examine facts to discover the truth
Make sense	Come to a logical explanation or understanding
Persuade	Convince someone of your way of thinking
Question	Request information or an answer
Reflect	Think deeply about something or someone
Refute	Prove something is wrong
Share	Give something to or experience something with others

Important inquiry concepts	
Assumption	A belief something is true although there is no proof
Bias	Favouritism for or against something or someone
Curiosity	Desire to learn more about something
Feedback	Information that is used for the basis of improvement
Flexible	Willing to change or try different things
Implication	Possible effect or result of an action
Inquiry	Asking about and investigating questions and problems
Metacognition	Thinking about thinking, knowing about knowing
Open-minded	Willing to consider different ideas and opinions
Perspective	Mental view or outlook
Perseverance	Continuing to try even though it is difficult
Point of view	Particular attitude or way of thinking
Risk	Possibility something will fail
Self-confidence	Confidence in your powers and abilities
Wonder	Surprise caused by something beautiful, unfamiliar or inexplicable

Words to describe thoughts, feelings and beliefs	
Abstract	Not a physical object, typically an idea
Accurate	Correct and true
Clear	Easy to understand, not confusing
Coherent	Logical and consistent
Concept	An idea of what something is or how it works
Effective	Able to get things done
Ethical	Beliefs about what is right and wrong
Logical	Clear, sound thinking, sensible and reasonable
Practical	Likely to succeed if tried, real not abstract
Precise	Exact, accurate, careful
Relevant	Closely connected to the topic or question
Reliable	Trustworthy, dependable
Significant	Important enough to be noticed or have an effect

Student exploration: Can you identify an argument?

Name: _____ Date: _____

Arguments are the ways in which we try to present our thinking to the world and convince others that our view is correct. Arguments do not have to involve anger and yelling. Creating an argument is simply the way we reason or think through a question or problem.

Arguments have two main components: a belief followed by the reasons we believe. Arguments are different than explanations, opinions or descriptions.

Take a look at the statements below and decide which ones are arguments. You may also notice that some arguments are stronger than others. Try to think why that is.

1. It is extremely windy today. I better wear a coat since it's so far to the bus stop.

2. The rule about not being able to eat lunch in the hallway is unfair. I want it to change.

3. People can be really rude and inappropriate on social media. Since young children can't understand what is being said or would be hurt by what is said, you should be at least 10 years old before using social media and even then, they should have their parent's permission.

4. The reason space exploration is challenging is because it's expensive to create technology that allows humans to live in space.

5. If boys and girls have equal skill in sports, then there should be a cricket team for girls as well as boys.

6. The milk reached the boiling point at 105 degrees Celsius.

7. All students should be treated the same and all students have the right to succeed in school. But some learners have different needs in order to learn to read, write or do math. That is why it is fair to allow some learners more time, a computer or an assistant to help them at school.

Reproducible 2G

Student exploration: Errors in thinking and logic

Name: _____ Date: _____

Take a look at the following examples of errors in thinking and logic. Explain what seems "wrong" or "weak" about the thinking.

Statement	Thinking error analysis
He has no children of his own, so his ideas on how to improve schools can't be right.	
She's such a nice and friendly person. She must have good ideas.	
Everyone says this is the best way, so I do it this way too.	
A boy must have vandalized this locker.	
All my friends say I'm right. Your friends think you are right. I have more friends than you, so I'm right.	
I was just thinking about you when you texted me. We must have a psychic connection.	
I really enjoy fishing. My parents enjoy fishing. So no one could object to fishing.	
I don't care about the evidence that it's unhealthy; I'm entitled to my own opinion and I think it's healthy.	
I'll be really offended if you disagree with my idea!	
Go ahead, prove that I am wrong!	

Teacher checklist: Purposeful planning for inquiry

Check which of the following statements represents how you plan for inquiry learning. Use this checklist for self-reflection, planning and sharing with colleagues, and to determine your next steps in deepening inquiry practice.

- I design learning tasks connected to essential questions in students' lives, subject disciplines and to the world while focusing on clear and achievable learning targets.

- I design inquiry tasks that allow for optimal student autonomy and appropriate cognitive demand.

- I establish classroom conditions that support inquiry (e.g., purposeful student talk, individual reflective thinking, honouring student interests and experiences).

- My learning tasks and assessment plan detail inquiry learning opportunities based on the distinct stages of an inquiry process.

- My learning tasks and assessment plan promote growth in inquiry dispositions (e.g., curiosity, perseverance, risk-taking, open-mindedness).

- My learning tasks and assessment plan balance inquiry learning opportunities in addition to other learning opportunities.

- I have opportunities to co-plan, co-teach and co-assess inquiry learning activities and products with colleagues.

- I have resources that support my learning in inquiry-based pedagogies.

- Parents and community members will be apprised of and included in inquiry learning.

Student exploration: KWHLAQ chart

Name: _____   Date: _____

Key questions		My thinking
K	What do I **KNOW**?	
W	What do I **WANT** to know?	
H	**HOW** do I find out?	
L	What have I **LEARNED**?	
A	What **ACTION** will I take?	
Q	What **QUESTIONS** do I have?	

Reproducible 3B
Student exploration: Why question?

Name: _____ Date: _____

I asked questions (today/this week) because I wanted to:

- get some information
- explore and investigate further
- clarify something that was confusing to me
- show that I'm doubtful about something I read or heard
- toss ideas around or brainstorm ideas and possibilities
- get another opinion or some advice
- debate, argue or dispute something I read or heard
- challenge some facts or an argument
- inquire about what other people felt or thought

Here are some of my questions...

_____

_____

_____

I think my questions are relevant because...

_____

_____

_____

I could improve my questioning by...

_____

_____

_____

Student exploration: Asking questions arising from provocations

Name: _____ Date: _____

Inquiry focus: _____

Work in your group to create inquiry questions based on the provocation provided.

1. Have a discussion about what you observed or experienced.

    a. What do we see?_____

    b. What is it or what is happening? _____

    c. Why was it made or why is it happening?_____

2. Each person in the group writes down 1–2 questions about what they see.

    My 1st question: _____

    My 2nd question: _____

3. After everyone has 1–2 questions, as a group, choose the one question you are most curious about and "perfect" it into an inquiry question your group would like to answer.

    Our inquiry question: _____

4. Does our question meet these criteria for an inquiry question?

    • We will have to think hard to answer it.

    • We won't find the answer just by looking at a website.

    • There is no one "correct" answer but many possible answers.

    • We will have to have good reasons for our answer.

    • We are really curious about it and want to find out more.

    • We haven't really thought about this before.

    • We feel strongly about our question.

    • It makes us think of more questions.

Student exploration: What I see, what I think, what I wonder, what I feel

Name: _____ Date: _____

Inquiry focus: _____

In each of the spaces record what you see, think, wonder and feel about your inquiry.

What do I see?

What do I think?

What do I wonder?

What do I feel?

Assessment planning template: Asks questions

Name: _____ Date: _____

Essential inquiry ability — Asking questions	Evidence gathered		
	Conversations	Observations	Products
Asks questions • Asks and refines relevant questions for different purposes (to get information, to clarify, to dispute, to drive an inquiry) and from different perspectives.			
Demonstrates curiosity • Actively asks many questions that demonstrate eagerness to learn. • Understands the importance of questioning to learning.			
(Gives and) Asks for reasons • Asks for justification of beliefs, proposals and solutions. • Thinks together. • Listens to, builds on, considers and assists with the questions of others. • Asks relevant questions of other people to further an inquiry (to get an opinion or some advice, to debate, to dispute, to inquire, to brainstorm).			
Understands what is currently known • Asks critical questions of "what is already known" (i.e., sources, data, strategies, theories).			
Puts it all together • Asks and understands the importance of analytical questions to improve their thinking at each stage of an inquiry.			

Inquiry rubric and self-check: Asks questions

Name: _____   Date: _____

Areas that need work	Standard for this criteria	How work exceeds expectations
	Asks questions • Asks and refines relevant questions for different purposes (to get information, to clarify, to dispute, to drive an inquiry) and from different perspectives.	
	Demonstrates curiosity • Actively asks questions that demonstrate eagerness to learn.	
	(Gives and) Asks for reasons • Asks for justification of beliefs, proposals and solutions.	
	Thinks together • Listens to, builds on, considers and assists with the questions of others. • Asks relevant questions of other people to further an inquiry (to get an opinion or some advice, to debate, to dispute, to inquire, to brainstorm).	
	Understands what is currently known • Asks critical questions of "what is already known" (i.e., sources, data, strategies, theories).	
	Puts it all together • Asks and understands the importance of analytical questions to improve their thinking at each stage of an inquiry.	

SOURCE: This single-point rubric is based on ideas from Jennifer Gonzalez's blog Brilliant or Insane: Education on the Edge, "Your Rubric is a Hot Mess; Here's How to Fix It."

Teacher checklist: Curiosity and questions in my classroom

Check which of the following statements represents your teaching practice. The focus of this checklist is questioning, an essential quality of inquiry thinking. Use this checklist for self-reflection, planning and sharing with colleagues, and to determine next steps in deepening inquiry practice.

- Students' questions are taken up in meaningful ways in my classroom.

- Students get to practise asking different types of questions in my classroom.

- Students understand why asking questions is important to learning in general, and inquiry learning in particular.

- Students in my classroom know there are different types of questions with different purposes and apply this knowledge.

- Students pose questions (including inquiry questions) and real world problems that relate to their lives and the "real world."

- Students ask analytical questions of their thinking during an inquiry.

- Students understand the criteria for effective questioning and can effectively self- and peer-assess questions.

- I use a variety of provocations to pique and sustain student curiosity, wonder and questioning.

- I pose questions and/or real world problems that relate to students' lives and the "real world."

- I pose questions and/or real world problems to provoke student curiosity and accelerate students' desire to learn.

- I organize factual knowledge around conceptual frameworks and open-ended inquiry questions to facilitate knowledge retrieval and application.

- I pose analytical questions to help students improve their thinking.

- I pose instructional questions to reveal students' prior knowledge, including preconceptions and misconceptions regarding important concepts.

- I assess students' questioning abilities through conversations, observations and products.

"Open for learning" sign

Evaluating sources and evidence: P.A.S.S.

Name: _____   Date: _____

Inquiry focus: _____

Evidence being evaluated: _____

Key questions		My evaluation of the evidence
P	**PURPOSE** Why and when was it created? Is it important to my inquiry?	
A	**ACCURACY** Is the information correct, truthful and unbiased? Should I use it?	
S	**SOURCE** Who created it? Are they an expert? Are they believable?	
S	**SUPPORT** Is it supported by other information and sources? What does this tell me?	

Evaluating sources and evidence: U.S.E. I.T.

Name: _____   Date: _____

Inquiry focus: _____

Evidence being evaluated: _____

Key questions		My evaluation of the evidence
U	**USEFULNESS** How will it help me answer my question? How important is it?	
S	**SOURCE** Where did it come from? When was it created? Is it the original or has it been changed?	
E	**EVIDENCE** Is it supported by other evidence? What does it tell me?	
I	**IMPARTIAL** Is it fair and unbiased? Who created it? Why did they create it?	
T	**THINKING** Does it change my thinking? What does it tell me?	

Adapted from work developed by Jesse Denison and David Nolan during the York University certificate course in Inquiry-Based Learning (Spring 2015).

Assessment planning template: Understands what is currently known

Name: _____ Date: _____

Essential inquiry ability — Understands what is currently known	Evidence gathered		
	Conversations	Observations	Products
Asks questions • Asks and refines relevant questions about the reliability, usefulness, authority and bias of evidence.			
Demonstrates curiosity • Actively asks many questions during the investigative stage. • Demonstrate an eagerness to explore, find things and learn.			
(Gives and) Asks for reasons • Asks for justification of a particular argument or position taken in a piece of evidence.			
Understands what is currently known • Has the necessary facts and information. • Is able to understand different perspectives within a body of evidence.			
Puts it all together • Understands when "enough" evidence has been collected and/or considered.			
Thinks together • Listens to, builds on, considers and assists others during the investigative process. • Asks relevant questions of other people to further an inquiry (gets an opinion or some advice, debates, disputes, inquires, brainstorms).			

Inquiry rubric and self-check: Understands what is currently known

Name: _____ Date: _____

Areas that need work	Standard for this criteria	How work exceeds expectations
	Asks questions • Asks and refines relevant questions about the reliability, usefulness, authority and bias of evidence.	
	Demonstrates curiosity • Actively asks many questions during the investigative stage. • Demonstrate an eagerness to explore, find things and learn.	
	(Gives and) Asks for reasons • Asks for justification of a particular argument or position taken in a piece of evidence.	
	Understands what is currently known • Has the necessary facts and information. • Is able to understand different perspectives within a body of evidence.	
	Puts it all together • Understands when "enough" evidence has been collected and/or considered.	
	Thinks together • Listens to, builds on, considers and assists others during the investigative process. • Asks relevant questions of other people to further an inquiry (gets an opinion or some advice, debates, disputes, inquires, brainstorms).	

This single-point rubric is based on ideas from Jennifer Gonzalez's Blog Brilliant or Insane: Education on the Edge, "Your Rubric is a Hot Mess; Here's How to Fix It."

Teacher checklist: Investigative mindset in my classroom

Check which of the following statements represents your current teaching practice. The focus of this checklist is on the investigative step of the inquiry process. You may want to use this checklist for self-reflection, for planning and sharing with colleagues, and to determine next steps in deepening inquiry practice.

- An investigative mindset is fostered in meaningful ways in my classroom.

- Conditions in my classroom encourage an investigative mindset.

- I purposefully plan our classroom experiences to minimize the impact of preconceptions and misconceptions.

- I locate age- and grade-appropriate resources for my students to drive their inquiry learning.

- I make sure that students are exposed to multiple perspectives during their inquiries.

- Students know that they cannot draw a conclusion before they have considered multiple perspectives.

- Students are learning how to determine the quality of sources.

- I know how to facilitate the investigative portion of an inquiry.

- I use a variety of provocations to pique and sustain student curiosity, wonder and questioning during the inquiry.

- I build in collaboration opportunities during the investigative phase of inquiry.

Student exploration: Making sense of my inquiry

Name: _____ Date: _____

Inquiry focus: _____

Question	My response
What do I think I might find?	
What did I find?	
What did I find that surprised me?	
What trends or patterns exist?	
Can I draw connections between ideas?	
What might have I overlooked?	
What conclusion(s) can I draw from this evidence?	
What questions remain? What new questions do I have?	
How might I explore this further?	

Student self-check: Making sense

Name: _____ Date: _____

Inquiry focus: _____

Self-check: The synthesis process	Yes	Mostly	A little	Not yet
I made thoughtful conclusions based on my research.				
I talked about my research and my conclusions with my group or peers.				
I wrote down useful feedback from my group and peers.				
I used that feedback to improve my conclusion.				

Credit: Sonia Racco, York Region District School Board. Work completed as part of Inquiry-Based Learning Module, July 2015. Toronto, Ontario.

PMI Chart

Name: _____ Date: _____

Inquiry focus: _____

Use this template to help you draw a conclusion about the question you are investigating.

+
Evidence that SUPPORTS my conclusion

Evidence that DOES NOT support my conclusion
—

Other interesting evidence I uncovered

Balance of evidence

Name: _____   Date: _____

Evidence for conclusion A	Evidence for conclusion B

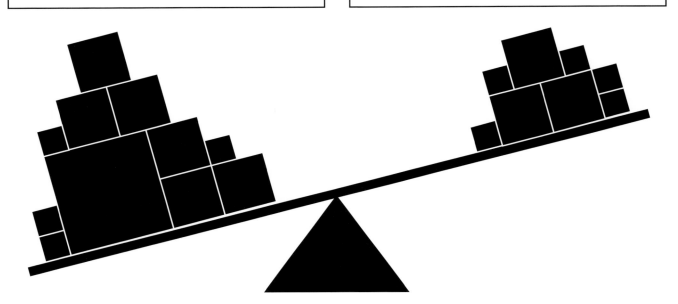

1. When drawing a conclusion, we shouldn't just look at the amount of evidence that supports one side or another of an inquiry; we should also examine the quality of evidence. Do you have some evidence you think is of better quality than other pieces of evidence? How much weight do you give to those pieces of evidence?

2. What about evidence that supports another conclusion? Does that mean you shouldn't consider the evidence? Or does it mean that your response to the inquiry question might be "There doesn't seem to be a definitive answer to the inquiry question..."

Assessment planning template: Puts it all together

Name: _____ Date: _____

Essential inquiry ability — Puts it all together	Evidence gathered		
	Conversations	Observations	Products
Asks questions • Asks and refines relevant questions about a body of evidence, inconsistencies in the evidence, and the weight of different pieces of evidence.			
Demonstrates curiosity • Actively asks many questions during synthesis and consolidation that demonstrate eagerness to learn.			
(Gives and) Asks for reasons • Asks for justification of evidence and gives reasons for a conclusion.			
Understands what is currently known • Is able to synthesize/consolidate "what is already known" (i.e., facts, data, theories).			
Puts it all together • Can synthesize a body of evidence into a coherent "whole." • Looks for patterns and trends in evidence. • Makes connections between ideas.			
Thinks together • Listens to, builds on, considers and assists others during the synthesis process. • Asks relevant questions of other people to further an inquiry (gets an opinion or some advice, debates, disputes, inquires, brainstorms).			

Inquiry rubric and self-check: Puts it all together

Name: _____ Date: _____

Areas that need work	Standard for this criteria	How work exceeds expectations
	Asks questions • Asks and refines relevant questions for different purposes (about a body of evidence, about inconsistencies in evidence, about the weight of different pieces of evidence) and from different perspectives.	
	Demonstrates curiosity • Actively asks many questions during synthesis and consolidation that demonstrate eagerness to learn.	
	(Gives and) Asks for reasons • Asks for justification of evidence and gives reasons for a conclusion.	
	Understands what is currently known • Is able to synthesize/consolidate "what is already known" (i.e., sources, data, strategies, theories).	
	Puts it all together • Can synthesize a body of evidence into a coherent "whole." • Looks for patterns and trends in evidence. • Makes connections between ideas.	
	Thinks together • Listens to, builds on, considers and assists others during the synthesis process. • Asks relevant questions of other people during the synthesis process (gets an opinion or some advice, debates, disputes, inquires, brainstorms).	

Teacher checklist: Synthesis and consolidation in my classroom

Check which of the following statements represents your current teaching practice. The focus of this checklist is on the consolidation step of the inquiry process. You may want to use this checklist for self-reflection, for planning and sharing with colleagues, and to determine next steps in deepening inquiry practice.

- Synthesis and consolidation skills are fostered in meaningful ways in my classroom.

- Conditions in my classroom encourage the development of synthesis and consolidation skills.

- I purposefully plan our classroom experiences to minimize the impact of brain errors on the synthesis and consolidation phase of inquiry.

- I use age- and grade-appropriate templates to drive the inquiry learning of my students.

- I make sure that students have considered multiple perspectives while consolidating their evidence.

- Students know that not all evidence is of equal weight.

- Students are learning how to weigh both the amount and quality of evidence while drawing a conclusion.

- I know how to facilitate the synthesis portion of an inquiry.

- I use a variety of provocations to pique and sustain student curiosity, wonder and questioning during the synthesis phase of inquiry.

- I build in collaboration opportunities during the synthesis phase of inquiry.

Conclusion of inquiry: Student self-reflection

Name: _____ Date: _____

Self-reflection questions	My response
The inquiry question I explored	
The conclusion I reached	
Reasons for my conclusion (evidence)	
Is there an alternate conclusion I could have reached? If so, what is it? If not, why not?	
What questions remain?	

Pushing thinking deeper: Self-reflection prompts

Name: _____ Date: _____

Thoughts about my inquiry	
I'm confused by . . .	
I'm imagining that . . .	
I'm "re-thinking" . . .	
I made a good choice because . . .	
I have a valid conclusion because . . .	
The easiest part of my inquiry was . . .	
The hardest part of my inquiry was . . .	
I may have made a mistake when I . . .	
I probably should have done this one thing differently . . .	
I think I am now much better at . . .	
I am left with these questions . . .	
Next time I want to explore . . .	

Critique prompts: Peer feedback

Name: _____ Date: _____

Student I am critiquing: _____

Important points

- Remember to smile and nod your head while the other student is speaking/presenting.
- Don't give too much feedback during the critique (pick 3 or 4 things from this sheet).
- Only comment on things that will help the student to learn and do better.
- Thank the person for sharing with you!

Things I might say or ask during the critique	My ideas about their inquiry
I learned this from your inquiry . . . presentation/ blog/artwork/invention/solution/etc.	
What if . . . you asked this question/you found more sources/you changed this part?	
I have a similar question/idea/problem! Did you notice that . . . ?	
One thing I wonder is . . . ?	
What do you think should be done about this?	
What questions do you still have?	
What did you learn?	

SOURCES

Chapter 1

Adapted from Brunner, Cornelia. Inquiry-Process Model. Cited in *YouthLearn* (2012). Retrieved from http://www.youthlearn.org/learning/planning/lesson-planning/how-inquiry/how-inquiry

Friesen, Sharon and David Scott. Inquiry-based learning: A Review of the Research Literature. Paper prepared for the Alberta Ministry of Education, June 2013. Retrieved from https://inspiring.education.alberta.ca/wp-content/uploads/2014/04/Inquiry-Based-Learning-A-Review-of-the-Research-Literature.pdf

Polya, George. *How To Solve It*, 2nd ed., Princeton University Press, 1957.

Chapter 2

Lipman, Matthew. *Philosophy Goes to School*, Philadelphia: Temple University Press, 1988.

Lipman, Matthew. *Thinking in Education*, 2nd ed., New York: Cambridge University Press, 2003.

Chapter 3

Barell, John. *Developing More Curious Minds*, Association for Supervision and Curriculum Development, 2003.

McTighe, Jay and Grant Wiggins. *Essential Questions: Opening doors to student understanding*, Association for Supervision and Curriculum Development, 2013.

Paul, Richard and Linda Elder. *The Miniature Guide to the Art of Asking Questions*, Tomales, CA: Foundation for Critical Thinking, 2010.

Versteeg, Bryan and Mars One, www.marsone.com.

Chapter 4

Adapted from Bonesteel, Sarah. *Canada's Relationship with Inuit: A History of Policy and Program Development.* Courtesy of Aboriginal Affairs and Northern Development Canada, 2006.

Dufault, Carolyn. "Are you with me? Measuring student attention in the classroom." Washington University in St. Louis: The Teaching Centre, retrieved July 24, 2015.

Katz, Steven and Lisa Ain Dack. *Intentional Interruption: Breaking Down Learning Barriers to Transform Professional Practice.* Thousand Oaks, CA: Corwin Press, 2013.

Museum of Civilization, Inuit Identification Disc (1950), IV-C-4497, D2002-013314, CD2002-346.

Rogers, Sarah. "Kuujjuaq woman brings back symbol of the Inuit past", *Nunatsiaq News*, December 4, 2013.

Chapter 5

Cipriano, Michael and Thomas S. Gruca. "The Power of Priors: How Confirmation Bias Impacts Market Prices", *The Journal of Prediction Markets*, November 2015.

Donohoo, Jennifer. *Collaborative Inquiry for Educators. A Facilitator's Guide to School Improvement.* Thousand Oaks, CA: Corwin, 2013.

Hinn, Jenny. Grade 4 Light and Sound Unit: Before and After. Work completed as part of an Inquiry-Based Learning Module taken during July 2015. Toronto, Ontario.

Katz, Steven and Lisa Ain Dack. *Intentional Interruption: Breaking Down Learning Barriers to Transform Professional Practice.* Thousand Oaks, CA: Corwin Press, 2013.

Morrison, Karin, Ritchart, Ron and and Mark Church. *Making Thinking Visible: How to Promote Engagement, Understanding, and Independence for All Learners.* John Wiley and Sons, 2011.

Racco, Sonia. Self-Check Template: The Synthesis Process. Work completed as part of an Inquiry-Based Learning Module taken during July 2015. Toronto, Ontario.

Watt, Jennifer and Jill Colyer. *IQ: A Practical Guide to Inquiry-Based Learning.* Toronto: Oxford University Press, 2014.

Chapter 6

Watt, Jennifer and Jill Colyer. *IQ: A Practical Guide to Inquiry-Based Learning.* Toronto: Oxford University Press, 2014.

Reproducibles

1E Adapted from the research of Virginia S. Lee, *What is Inquiry-Guided Learning?* 2012.

2A Adapted from J. Walsh and B. Sattes, *Thinking Through Quality Questioning*, Corwin Press (2011).

3F Adapted from Jennifer Gonzalez's blog Brilliant or Insane: Education on the Edge, "Your Rubric is a Hot Mess; Here's How to Fix It."

4C Adapted from work developed by Jesse Denison and David Nolan during the York University certificate course in Inquiry-Based Learning (Spring 2015).

4E Adapted from Jennifer Gonzalez's Blog Brilliant or Insane: Education on the Edge, "Your Rubric is a Hot Mess; Here's How to Fix It."

Index